Taking Liberties

Taking Liberties

Satirical Prints of the French Revolution

JEAN-PAUL PITTION

French Bicentenary Committee, 1989

Ce livre est dédié à Aideen, François, Etienne et Una

*First published in 1989 by the
French Bicentenary Committee
18 Lakelands Avenue,
Kilmacud, Co. Dublin.*

*© Text: Jean-Paul Pittion
© Prints: Chester Beatty Library*

ISBN 0 9515096 08

*Printed by Irish Printers Ltd,
Clonshaugh Industrial Estate,
Dublin 17, Ireland*

"They made the walls of Paris didactic, suasive, with an ever-fresh Periodical Literature, wherein he that ran might read: Placard Journals, Placard Lampoons, Municipal Ordinances, Royal Proclamations; the whole other or vulgar Placard-department superadded, – or omitted from contempt! What unutterable things the stone-walls spoke, during these five years."

Thomas Carlyle.
The French Revolution.

Caricatures and satirical prints are a powerful medium through which the little man can strike back. It is a way of getting your own back on the system by sending it up through ridicule. *Taking Liberties* is a look at just under a hundred and thirty caricatures which depict another side or sides to the French Revolution. As heads rolled and the old system crumbled the artists/engravers who produced these prints give us a powerful interpretation of the grim realities of the Revolution. Masters of the *double entendre* they temper their political comment with wit and humour, and their engravers' burr spares no one, as Monarchy, clergy and bourgeois fall prey to their acid comment.

The range of material in *Taking Liberties* crosses boundaries of class and creed and mocks, gently or fiercely at both artistic conventions and the trappings of power. Behind the fighting and political posings depicted in the prints is the satirist's keen eye and irreverent, fresh outlook on life. Most of the caricatures have immediate impact, but some of the jokes have been lost in the mists of two hundred years. To this end Jean-Paul Pittion has applied himself and his scholarship to providing the key to unlock, through his detailed descriptions and analysis of the prints, the storehouse of laughter and humour.

All the caricatures and satirical prints are the property of Sir Alfred Chester Beatty, one of the last great collectors of the twentieth century. They were left as a part of the Beatty bequest when in 1968 he willed his collection to the Irish people. This is the first time they have been exhibited and are a part of Ireland's contribution to the world-wide celebrations to mark the Bicentenary of the French Revolution of 1789. As a private collector, Sir Alfred Chester Beatty did not keep records of his earlier purchases, and so we have no clue as to the provenance of this remarkable collection of ephemeral prints. It is most likely that they were purchased in France, as Beatty spent most of the winters of his life there. Certainly they have not seen the light of day for at least one hundred years, and their startlingly bright colours and fresh condition bear witness to this. In 1837 when he was writing his *French Revolution* Carlyle bemoans the fact that such material was "rotting slowly in the Public Libraries of our Europe." It is good to be able to prove the eminent gentleman wrong, at least in this instance.

Pat Donlon.
Director, National Library of Ireland and Trustee of the Chester Beatty Library.

ACKNOWLEDGEMENTS

Many people helped in many different ways towards the preparation of this book.

For financial support and faith in the project, our thanks go to H.E. the French Ambassador, Monsieur Jean Max Bouchaud, to Monsieur Denis Evesque, Cultural Counsellor at the French Embassy and to the Franco-Irish Bicentenary Committee, Dublin, and *Mission du Bicentenaire*, Paris. To Joseph Lynch, Department of Foreign Affairs, whose *sang froid* and support kept us going, our thanks.

We acknowledge our debt to the Trustees of the Chester Beatty Library for permission to reproduce the prints. Thanks also are due to the Director, Wilfrid Lockwood, to Vera Grief, and to all the security staff at the Library, and in particular Christy Hoey. William Aliaga Kelly gave generously of his time and skills.

For the printing of the book – a painstaking and tricky business at the best of times – but particularly so in the case of eighteenth-century hand-coloured prints and fine aquatints, we owe special thanks to Irish Printers Ltd., and in particular to Peter O'Connell and Anita Masterson. We are grateful to the Managing Director and staff of Ultragraphics for their infinite patience in the making of photographic plates, and in particular to Hilary Cooke,

Susan Costello and John Hegerty. Thanks are due to the designer of the book Bill Bolger for constant advice, solace and sheer good humour, and also to the staff of the National College of Art and Design.

To Charles Benson, Aine Keegan and the staff of the Department of Older Printed Books, Trinity College, Dublin, whose professionalism was tested and not found wanting, our thanks. We are grateful to the French Department, TCD, Professor Roger Little, and in particular Anne Burke for patient typing of text and to Professor Barbara Wright for unfailing encouragement. We are grateful also to the Faculty of Arts (Letters) TCD, and to Richard Cox and Vivienne Jenkins for their support. A special word of thanks is due to Jacqueline Clarke for observations, advice and help.

All scholars depend on the helpfulness and resources of libraries and collections, and we are grateful to the staff of Bibliothèque de l'Arsenal and Cabinet des Estampes, Bibliothèque Nationale, Paris; Archives de la Ville de Paris; Musée Pédagogique, Paris; and the National Library of Ireland.

For expert advice freely given thanks to John McCormick, TCD, Fintan Cullen, TCD, and Hugh Gough, UCD.

For practical assistance our thanks

to Robin Moore and Hunter Advertising, Brian Maguire for the poster design and House of Piat for sponsoring it. John Farrell, Eugene Hogan, Peter Kenny and Donall Ó Luanaigh of the National Library gave generously of their time. We owe special thanks to the staff of Allied Irish Banks, Ranelagh, in particular Peter Gaughan and Oliver Williams.

Finally there were certain individuals who helped in countless ways: Jan Winter, Sylvia Batt, Paulyn Marrinan, Eugene McCarthy, Dublin and Jean-Michel, Berenice and Nicole Galano, Paris. Deirdre O'Regan was a quiet, efficient and ever courteous presence – our thanks to her and to the Arts Administration Course UCD, for allowing us to avail of her skills.

Pat Donlon, NLI
Jean-Paul Pittion, TCD

One of the last decrees adopted by the Constituent Assembly in September 1791 was the allocation of a special subsidy of one hundred thousand *livres*. Special purchases relating to the Revolution were to form part of the newly created Bibliothèque Nationale. D'Ormesson, the first librarian, needed the money to increase a collection which he had begun, and which was intended to preserve for posterity as many "fugitive pieces" relating to the Revolution as possible. He wrote that it was 'indispensable' to do so without delay, for such pieces can only be acquired when they are new. By 1792 the collection already numbered some 11496 pieces, including 3416 prints which he assembled in 18 portfolios.

D'Ormesson's project is significant in two respects: first it is indicative of the sheer volume of the print production in the early days of the Revolution. In fact, the collections of Musée Carnavalet which concern largely Paris, number some 4000 pieces covering the decade of the Revolution. To this must be added the many prints produced by provincial print makers, *dominotiers, cartiers,* particularly those of Orléans.

D'Ormesson's project is also significant of a new approach to prints and their role during the Revolution. His 18 portfolios were arranged by subject matter into 26 sections following a rough chronological and alphabetical order. The prints were to be treated as illustrating or commenting upon "any person or event" cited "in any manner whatsoever by journalists or pamphleteers". Æsthetic criteria were not relevant. Prints should be gathered "whether good or bad".

In 1808, during the Empire, a member of the *Institut de France*, Le Breton, produced a report for Napoleon on the state of the graphic arts in France during the previous twenty years. D'Ormesson's "sequence of historical pieces until April 1793" is only mentioned in a footnote to the report. Le Breton is interested in 'quality' or high art prints. Regarding those in this category which were published during the Revolution, Le Breton is critical of the choice of subject, regretting the relative absence of the grand historical genre. He concentrates on line engravings and etchings, ignores aquatint and disparages stipple. He judges beauty on the basis of skill and technique, retaining the pre-revolutionary concept of taste to praise or criticise. An appeal to æsthetics enables him to dismiss (with the begrudging exception of *Tableaux Historiques*) most of the political prints produced during the Revolution.

In times of Revolution all art is in a sense political and many of the established genres of graphic art underwent a process of politicization during the decade 1789-1799. Portraiture, allegory, commemorative or narrative tableaux, even genre scenes and art interpretation can be said to have been in "semi-revolution". There is however one genre which emerges during that period and is above all others significant of the change brought about by the politics of the period: satirical and polemical prints destined to a broad audience. Relatively cheaply produced (either in aquatint or in hand-coloured etchings), these prints are, as D'Ormesson understood, the graphic equivalent of the political press. The few contemporary sources which mention them, call them "caricatures", though in the tradition this should be reserved for personal *portraits-charge*. We shall call them cartoons, despite the obvious anachronistic connotations of the term, as they comment in a humorous vein on a wide variety of subjects, all of them topical and political. The fullest list available to date (Blum's) numbers some 600 titles. This represents a small proportion of all prints produced during the Revolutionary decade. Issued in editions of between three and five hundred copies, widely distributed and shown in print shops, the impact of these cartoons on public opinion was considerable however, as contemporary reactions to them show. They come nearest to being, in the words of Lynn Hunt, a new political mass media. The Chester Beatty Library collection is amongst the richest outside France. The selection we now present is representative of the ingenuity and of the variety of political viewpoints of the mostly anonymous artists who produced them.

The view of politics and of history that is presented in the cartoons, is not however as chronologically straightforward as D'Ormesson had assumed. When we date them from internal and, when available, external evidence and treat them as historical series, it is obvious that their production had a tempo and requires a periodization of its own. In following the traditional order applied in national collections, and in assuming that these prints can be dated by reference to a particular occurrence or person upon which they comment, earlier studies have also distorted their impact. External sources which make accurate dating possible are unfortunately few. Amongst periodicals *Feuille du Libraire*, later *Feuille de Littérature* carries notices of publications only for a few cartoons. *Journal de la Cour et de la Ville*, and *Journal du Peuple*, provide crucial evidence for the dating of prints produced by Palais Royal print publishers, but only for the limited period of the Legislative Assembly (late 1791-mid 1792) and only for the right-wing production, particularly Webert's. In general, periodicals such as *Moniteur* are only interested in 'quality' prints. And until 1793 when *dépôt légal* was reorganized to protect literary and artistic property, print makers did not register their production. When a print is dated (as no. 62) it is in mock imitation of British regulations which did not apply in France.

Dating may help, but only interpretation of the context of publication reveals the role played by cartoons in shaping public opinion. Thus no. 75 in our list is announced as being on sale in *Journal de la Cour et de la Ville* in December 1791. Yet its subject matter is a report by Chabroud on the march on Versailles which occurred on 5-6 October 1789. The report itself was given to the Constituent Assembly a year after on 30 September 1790. Why does the cartoon appear so long after the events? In some cases (e.g. no. 71) it is probable that the periodical advertises a print published quite some time before, or a re-issue. But then why the re-issue? Comparison with closely related topics and subject matter shows that the two prints echo a campaign of vilification, inspired by the right-wing press and aimed at discrediting political figures associated with the previous two years of revolution at the start of the new Legislative Assembly.

Pro-revolutionary prints also comment on recurring topics, e.g. the abolition of privileges, the new Constitution, the Clergy and the Church. Many momentous measures of principle were adopted by the Assembly on these crucial issues in the second half of 1789, but debates on their implementation lasted over the next two years, as the Revolution generated a political momentum of its own which transformed many of these issues. As an example, no 48 comments on the subject of the property qualification for election candidates introduced by the Assembly in October 1788. The measure was adopted with little opposition, and it came under fire from clubs and popular societies only with the upsurge in popular politics which occurred early in 1791. The publication of the cartoon marks, in this case, the emergence of an issue, intensified by public debate.

Thus both right-wing and left-wing cartoons select their subject matter to suit political circumstances. They focus on a topic, an event or a political figure, according to the perception that their makers have of the issues of which a potential audience is most likely aware at a given time. And despite an obvious tendency to typify and deal more with general issues, left wing cartoons are in this regard no less topical. nos. 36 and 37, apparently general satires on the reactionary clergy, are in fact closely related to the resistance of high clergy *députés* to the constitutional oath, and to the role played by one of them, Abbé Maury, as the focus of this resistance.

The cartoons which appeared during the early years of the Revolution therefore give an oblique view of events, reflecting the reception of these events in public opinion. The perception of events was itself influenced by the comment on news which was an essential element of revolutionary political culture. The role played by the press in this culture was a major one, and cartoonists were often guided by it. Two important periodicals, Camille Desmoulins's *Révolutions de France et de Brabaut* and Gattey's *Actes des Apôtres*, included cartoons, and no doubt contributed to establish and popularise the genre. Most cartoons however were independent productions, providing an autonomous visual counterpoint to the press. A speech or a statement by a leading political figure published in the press, a witty or polemical comment by a journalist, the title of a polemical or satirical brochure provided the starting point. But the political culture in which they have their roots is that of political speech. A piece of hearsay, a rumour, a joke, words alleged to be spoken, a piece of gossip provided immediate inspiration for a number of our cartoons (see nos. 56, 63, 68, 76).

Cartoons were born out of occasion, but their choice of subject matter reflected what captured the political interest of their audience. The production is one of circumstance, but focused on issues and themes which feature prominently in public debates at the time when they appear.

Some productions, in particular a series of cartoons on the secularization of the clergy, simply reflect the entertainment which people got from a political victory. Others aimed more at propaganda: as well as echoing issues, they sought to raise them in the minds of their audience, to subvert the commitment of those engaged in revolutionary action, to demoralize, to generate rumour. Yet despite their potential, until the crisis of 1793-4, public authorities showed little interest in using graphic humour or satire as a means of propaganda.

In part official blindness must be due to the fact that, according to existing canons of taste, humour and satire were considered too low a register for the expression of civic values. In part also, it was respect for the freedom of expression. In the legacy of the *Ancien Régime* censorship and official sponsorship came together. The Crown seized and destroyed satirical prints attacking Church, Court and Government, though it allowed, encouraged and even sponsored satirical prints for instance topics, such as the expulsion of the Jesuits, or on international conflicts, or rival European powers. Early attempts at some new form of censorship, made by the provisional municipal government of Paris in July 1789, were quickly defeated, and the new régime refrained from positive (or negative) interference with the publication of prints which like printing were recognised to be, in the words of Millin, in his *Lettre aux Représentants de la Commune de Paris* the "means of rendering manifest" individual thoughts. Official commissioning of caricatures including two by David by the Committee of Public Safety in 1793 coincides with the reintroduction of controls on public opinion.

Though each satirical or polemical print of the period is an individual creation, the chronology of the production shows that it has an overall thematic structure: the image of the Revolution refracted by cartoons is that of issues or personalities, rather than ideals or events, as would be the case for the allegorical or commemorative production, to which the vast program of civic education undertaken by the Revolution was entrusted. The main themes of cartoons are provided by the October Days, the end of *privilégiés*, the secularization of the orders and resistance to the Constitutional church, the *emigré* leaders and their armies, the Papal Brief of 1791, the Flight to Varennes, the Champ de Mars affair, the financial crisis of 1791-2, the factional politics of the Legislative, the War, the Fall of the Monarchy. After August 1792, the trial of Louis and the clash of personalities in the Convention and the Committee of

Public Safety are favoured themes, and some particularly vengeful satires appear just after Thermidor.

———

Cartoons therefore appear together in clusters at particular critical times, forming a sequence of campaigns of public opinion. Not all of these campaigns were inspired by a concerted or deliberate political intention. Basset the print merchant from Rue Saint Jacques (see no. 24) was said to have become "big and fat" on the sales of his anti-clerical prints (see no. 28), many of which seek above all to entertain. Nevertheless most prints reveal a political intention.

Research on pro-revolutionary artists, Marie Anne Croisier, Villeneure or "AP", will show whether they produced their work on their own initiative or whether they were encouraged or even commissioned by clubs and societies. Boyer de Nîmes, always ready to spot a conspiracy, certainly thought so. Gautier, the editor of *Journal de la Cour et de la Ville*, encouraged and prompted at least some of the cartoons produced by Michel Webert at Palais Royal, and this association comes the closest to a deliberate anti-revolutionary campaign conducted jointly by the press and by print makers.

Undoubtedly these campaigns had their impact: prints were sold by street hawkers or in shops where they were displayed. They were pinned on walls in clubs, societies and in shops: a print by "AP" copied several times (cf Arsenal, 220 nos. 55-57) shows the interior of a cobbler's shop on the wall of which hangs another famous cartoon, "Les 3 Ordres". People reacted to all kinds of prints, and not always as intended. A police informer Beraud, reported in March 1793, that "muscadins" and "petites-maîtresses" bought engravings showing Le Peletier's and Marat's deaths to gloat over them. Gautier in his *Journal* warns his readers that Teroigne de Mericourt threatened a "marchande de caricatures" at Palais Royal, that she would come "with a few patriots" and tear into pieces anti-revolutionary prints for sale there. *Sections*, clubs and societies were often the initiators of searches in print-shops.

———

Unlike other genres, cartoons were not intended to convince or persuade, but as Boyer de Nîmes put it, to arouse political passions: the cartoons we show admonish, jeer, belittle, deride, insult or abuse. Some are political graffiti, but many are visual slogans and show a close relationship with all forms of political speech. Readability and adaptibility of design, instantaneity and simultaneity of message made them a form of political media particularly well suited to a mixed street audience where the totally illiterate rubbed shoulders with the sophisticated.

To achieve a common appeal, cartoons draw upon a rich visual rhetoric. Tropes are used to satirize political figures: they infantilize or animalize. After Varennes Louis is shown as a child playing with the toys of office. Animal tropes abound. The pig trope first applied by Villeneuve in a set of medalions in 1789 (see nos. 11-14) is particularly successful. Right-wing cartoonists turn La Fayette into a centaur, Narbonne into a linnet. Recurring tropes assign to their targets a *persona* which accompanies them from cartoon to cartoon. Once a turkey, Bailly the first mayor of Paris will always be a turkey.

Schemes combine with tropes to represent the political process. Some schemes, like scenes of devils taking their victims away are long established commonplaces, *topoi* dating back from Reformation satires. The suppression of privileges is shown in the form of mild or violent grooming: nails (or wings) are clipped, beards and heads shaved. Procedures from the technology of the times — pressing, levelling, weighing — are particularly effective in expressing political struggles.

Given the basic literacy of most of the audience, cartoons retain a close connection with the spoken word. Cartoons talk or babble (*he! hue! dada!*). They stage a dialogue, recite verse or song. Above all they express or translate into visual terms all forms of set utterances and of verbal humour: idioms, sayings, proverbs, puns and nicknames. Title and caption therefore are an essential part of the total image. Added lettering emphasizes the point, identifies the detail, provides additional clues. Some cartoons are in the format of a rebus, some in the manner of both verbal and visual puzzles. Word games and visual games are fully integrated in the most sophisticated examples (see no. 107).

———

Representation by contraries, exaggeration of detail, compression, displacement — all these techniques of wit and humour analysed by Freud are at work in producing the imagery of the cartoons. They reveal an obsessional interest in parts of the body (noses, stomachs, buttocks), a fascination for objects, the chain, the wheel, the blade, the stick, which belong to the language of a collective unconscious, the irrational behind the all too rational discourse of the Revolution.

Wit and humour, like dreams, are always culturally circumscribed. The pleasure which the audience drew from the cartoons was also one of sharing in the recognition of familiar images. For their designs the cartoons draw on a common visual as well as verbal lore. Eighteenth-century society lived in a highly

visual world: studies have shown that nearly half of ordinary Paris households owned some kind of print; shop-signs, displays, paintings in churches created a culture of fixed images, with an immediate awareness of many modes of pictorial and graphic representation. Spectacles, street shows, ceremonials of church or state heightened people's sense of performance. Clothes denoted rank and profession. The cartoons draw on this rich visual lore for their representations.

———

This common culture made it possible for the cartoons to address, through parody, audiences with various degrees of sophistication. The hand-coloured etchings produced by the Rue Saint Jacques trade during the Revolution are both satirical prints on topical subjects in the 'popular' manner and amusing take-offs of this 'popular' tradition in which the trade specialised. Palais Royal aquatints quote and parody known paintings, manners and genres; at the same time the central group of the cartoon is designed for immediate and broad recognition (see no. 74).

Ideology did influence aesthetics as it shaped satire: the humour of counter-revolutionary cartoons is more vindictive, more personalised, more literary; the graphic style is more elaborate in its detail — the format imitates architectural views, book

illustrations. Pro-revolutionary cartoons create types (e.g. *Le Père Duchesne*) or grotesques and use colour and outlines as in images prepared for magic lantern shows. However both sides borrowed ideas from each other if only to turn them around.

After Thermidor political comment gives way to social satire. The production of the early years of the Revolution however had established a genre. There were signs that an audience of connoisseurs was emerging: both Villeneuve in 1791 and Webert in 1792 launched collections of their "caricatures". The legacy of the Revolution, in this as in many other fields, was to mature during the next century.

J.P. Pittion
Trinity College, Dublin

REFERENCES

The prints are arranged in chronological order. In the list which follows each print is given its Accession number in the Chester Beatty Library collection (abbreviated as *CB AC.*). This is followed by the number in L.-F. Bruel's *Inventaire analytique de la Collection de Vinck* (3 vols, Paris 1909-1920) and in A. Blum's *La Caricature révolutionnaire* (Paris, 1916) — abbreviated as *DV* and *Blum*. In a few cases the reference is to other French national collections (e.g. Bibliothèque de l'Arsenal). In the technical descriptions an attempt has been made to express the intentions of the print makers as closely as possible: to this end different type faces are used to show variations in the lettering and a distinction is made between title and caption. Dimensions given are for plate (abbreviated *Pl.*) and design (*Des.*). Watermarks (*Wtmk*) and registration marks (*Reg. mks*) are noted. Wherever possible, the watermark is transcribed or identified. An * number indicates a colour plate to be found at the end of the volume.

A number of sources have been used for dating attribution and description: the most frequently quoted periodicals are *Journal de la Cour et de la Ville*, edited by Gautier, 1 Jan 1791–10 Aug 1792 (abbreviated *JCV*), *Journal du Peuple*, by Boyer de Nîmes, 1 Feb–12 Aug 1792 (*JP*), and *Feuille de Correspondance du Libraire*, known from September 1791 as *Feuille de Littérature*. Pamphlets and other contemporary printed sources are identified by their number in Tourneux's *Bibliographie de l'Histoire de Paris pendant la Révolution française* (5 vols, Paris 1890-1913) and in Martin and Walter's *Catalogue de l'Histoire de la Révolution française* (5 vols and *Table*, Paris, 1936-1943).

Of the earlier sources on the history of caricatures, the following have been used: Boyer de Nîmes, *Histoire de la Caricature de la Révolte des Français* (2 vols, Paris, 1792); A. Challamel, *Histoire-Musée de la République française depuis l'Assemblée des notables jusqu'à l'Empire* (3rd ed., 2 vols, Paris, 1857); J. Renouvier, *Histoire de l'Art pendant la Révolution*, Paris, 1863); J.-F. Champfleury, *Histoire de la Caricature* (Paris 1874).

A number of recent studies have been particularly helpful in guiding us in our interpretation, amongst these, contributions to the volume edited by M. Vovelle, *Les Images de la Révolution* (Paris 1988) and Lynn Hunt's stimulating article in vol 30 of *History To-day* (Oct. 1980) entitled "*Engraving the Republic: Prints and Propaganda in the French Revolution*".

The *Catalogue* of the Exhibition held in Musée Carnavalet in 1977, provides a useful guide to the many genres of prints produced during the Revolution. As our work was nearing completion, the commemorations of the Bicentenary led to the publication of a number of works and catalogues of exhibitions. Though most appeared too late to be taken into consideration, it is appropriate that they should be listed here: A. de Baecque, *La Caricature révolutionnaire*, Paris, CNRS 1988; J. Cuno and others, *Politique et polémique. La Caricature française et la Révolution*, University of California, Los Angeles, 1988; Cl. Langlois, *La Caricature contre-révolutionnaire*, Paris, CNRS, 1988; P. Jean-Richard, and G. Mondin, *Un Collectionneur pendant la Révolution: Jean Louis Soulavie (1752-1813)*, Paris, Musées Nationaux, 1989

A list of 128 cartoons in
The Chester Beatty Library

1	CB AC. 3027	DV 2077	Blum 60
2	CB AC. 3240		Blum 80
3	CB AC. 3213	DV 3908	Blum 11
4	CB AC. 3210	DV 3908	
5	CB AC. 3043	DV 2827	Blum 18
6	CB AC. 3037	DV 2819	Blum 35
7	CB AC. 3243		
8	CB AC. 3025		Blum 159
9	CB AC. 3242	DV 3539	Blum21
10	CB AC. 3196		cfBlum 209
11	CB AC. 3214	cfDV 1148	Blum 532
12	CB AC. 3215	cfDV 3923	
13	CB AC. 3216	cf DV 3921	
14	CB AC. 3217	cf DV 1149	
15*	CB AC. 3239	DV 3680	Blum 47
16	CB AC. 3241	DV 2814	Blum 72
17	CB AC. 3212		
18	CB AC. 3226		Blum 41
19	CB AC. 3036		
20	CB AC. 3194		
21	CB AC. 3222		
22	CB AC. 3208	cf DV 3078	Blum 136
23	CB AC. 3042	DV 1624	Blum 97
24*	CB AC. 3251	DV 3362	Blum 175
25	CB AC. 3199		
26	CB AC. 2838	DV 2669	Blum 359
27	CB AC. 3219		
28	CB AC. 3029	DV 3055	Blum 126
29	CB AC. 3198	DV 2734	Blum 140
30	CB AC. 3236		
31	CB AC. 3224		
32.	CB AC. 3223		Blum 342
33	CB AC. 3225		
34	CB AC. 3249	DV 3098	Blum 230
35*	CB AC. 3228		Blum 196
36	CB AC. 3250	DV 1331	Blum 428
37.	CB AC. 3197	DV 3096	Blum 230
38*	CB AC. 3038		Blum 379
39	CB AC. 3030	DV 4038	Blum 332
40	CB AC. 3035		Blum 125
41	CB AC. 3026		Blum 192
42	CB AC. 3248		Blum 229
43	CB AC. 3207	DV 3678	Blum 161
44	CB AC. 3220		Blum 260
45	CB AC. 3200	DV 3634	Blum 214
46*	CB AC. 3237	DV 3449	Blum 265
47	CB AC. 3202	DV 1633	Blum 98

48	CB AC.3221	DV 2747	Blum 117
49	CB AC. 3204		
50	CB AC. 3022	DV 3994	Blum 548
51*	CB AC. 3023		
52	CB AC. 3028	DV 3330	Blum 553
53*	CB AC 3245	DV 3979	
54	CB AC. 3209	DV 3927	Blum 281
55	CB AC. 3039	DV 3970	Blum 284
56	CB AC. 3041		
57	CB AC. 3021	DV 3930	Blum 276
58	CB AC. 3040	DV 3984	Blum 279
59	CB AC. 3201		
60	CB AC. 3211		
61*	CB AC. 3229	DV 3936	Blum 509
62	CB AC. 2996		
63	CB AC. 2982		
64	CB AC. 3206	DV 1842	Blum 398
65*	CB AC. 3238		
66	CB AC. 3195		
67	CB AC. 2841	DV 2968	Blum 362
68	CB AC. 2842	DV 1846	Blum 397
69	CB AC. 2833	Bibliothèque Nationale Qbl 101638	
70	CB AC. 2989		Blum 383
71	CB AC. 2837		Blum 396
72	CB AC. 2843	cf DV 1806	Blum 361
73	CB AC. 2844	DV 1806	Blum 361
74	CB AC. 2994	DV 3130	Blum 166
75	CB AC. 2991	DV 3020	Blum 445
76	CB AC. 2839	DV 4066	Blum 388
77	CB AC. 2855		Blum 310
78	CB AC. 2926	DV 4059	Blum 386
79	CB AC. 2846	DV 4278	Blum 312
80	CB AC. 2953		Blum 335
81	CB AC. 3007		
82	CB AC. 2993		Blum 448
83	CB AC. 3001	DV 2894	Blum 441
84*	CB AC. 3232		
85*	CB AC. 3227		
86	CB AC. 3205		Blum 510
87	CB AC. 2987	DV 1798	Blum 367
88	CB AC. 2832	DV 2975	Blum 110
89	CB AC. 2992		Blum 349
90	CB AC. 2957		Blum 619
91	CB AC. 2835	Bibliothèque Nationale Qbl 101104	
92	CB AC. 2974		Blum 350
93*	CB AC. 2997		Blum 454
94	CB AC. 2986		Blum 493
95	CB AC. 2859	DV 4310	Blum 311
96	CB AC. 2973	DV 3022	Blum 446
97	CB AC. 3006	DV 1803	Blum 373
98	CB AC. 2977	DV 4307	Blum 333
99	CB AC. 2969	Bibliothèque Nationale Qbl 101109	
100	CB AC. 2836	DV 5006	cf Blum 330
101	CB AC. 2984		Blum 403
102	CB AC. 2860	DV 3121	Blum 355
103	CB AC. 3018	DV 4313	Blum 323
104	CB AC. 2928		
105	CB AC. 2951		Blum 353
106	CB AC. 2950		
107	CB AC. 2956		Blum 572
108	CB AC. 2955		Blum 399
109	CB AC. 3008		Blum 582
110	CB AC. 2981		
111	CB AC. 2927		
112	CB AC. 2988	DV 3572	
113	CB AC. 2840		
114*	CB AC. 3015		Blum 444
115	CB AC. 2845	DV 1805	Blum 375
116	CB AC. 2985		
117	CB AC. 2970	cf DV 3132	Blum 168
118	CB AC. 2971	cf DV 3121	Blum 355
119*	CB AC. 3020		Blum 557
120	CB AC. 2976		Blum 461
121*	CB AC. 3231		
122	CB AC. 3024		
123	CB AC. 2856	DV 531	Blum 542
124	CB AC. 2952		Blum 357
125	CB AC. 2861	DV 4008	Blum 479
126	CB AC. 2857	Bibliothèque Nationale Qbl 101429	
127*	CB AC. 2990	DV 4007	Blum 480
128*	CB AC 3230		Blum 563

1

Untitled / *Sous la Gloire des Augustes Maisons de nos Princes, Minerve Deesse Protectrice de la France, Contemple le Tiers Etat figure par un laboureur poussant sa charrue dans un Sillon. De la Ceinture de ce Citoyen s'elevent des branches de Palmiers de Lauriers de Roses, d'ou sortent des Têtes d'Evêques, Moines, Cardinaux, Militaire et gens de Robe. La Vérité sortant d'un Nuage tient dans ses mains une Tête Couronnee etc*
Etching, hand coloured; Pl. 28, 3, 22, 1; Des. 25, 6 x 18, 2; Wtmk [Name MONB ... with hearts inserted]
Unsigned, undated [1789]

This allegory of the Tiers-Etat as the mainstay of the French nation and as the source of its wealth under the protection of the dynastic monarchy, is accompanied as usual by a long explanatory caption. The composition makes use of standard designs assembled in the shape of a garland, with at the top left hand side a constellation of sun and planets (to represent the French dynasty), in the foreground the two complementary figures of Minerva and the ploughman linked by plough and furrow, and at the top right hand side a strange *piece montée* in the shape of a bouquet from which emerge the heads of *privilégiés*. To this medley of all kinds of allegories and symbols, the designer has added, half hidden behind the clouds, the rear of a lion and the Fragonard like figure of a naked woman nursing what appears to be the representation of a King with crown (a timid reference to the state of the Kingdom at the time?). The background provides a symbolic context for the allegory. The rural scenery embodies an ideal vision of *Ancien Régime* society where the three 'estates' live in harmony (note the noble house, the cottage, the church spire) and wealth comes from the land: in the middle ground behind the ploughman, a field of corn is ripening.

Though giving pride of place to the Tiers-Etat the print does not attack the *privilégiés* or denounce the abuses of *Ancien Régime* society, as did many others which appeared on behalf of the *Tiers* during the convening and meeting of the Estates-General. It is either a clever piece of propaganda seeking to persuade rather than antagonize, or more probably, given its traditional language, a reformist statement, inspired by physiocratic ideals, and reflecting a long established liberal trend in *Ancien Régime* public opinion.

2

Untitled / HONNI SOIT QUI MAL Y VOIT.
Etching, hand coloured; Pl. 28,4 x 21,9; Des. 25,6 x 18,7; Wtmk
Unsigned, undated [early or mid 1789]

A proverb illustrated ("robbing the rich to give to the poor"), in the traditional genre derived from the Dutch tradition. A touch of fancy is introduced by the flirting group on the left. The print is interesting politically, as it shows the clergy taking from an aristocrat to give to the *Tiers Etat*. The theme appears in a number of other etchings, and clearly dates from the period of the end of the Estate General or the Constituant Assembly, when support from the lower clergy to the Tiers was a decisive factor.

Sous la Gloire des Augustes Maisons de nos Princes, Minerve Déesse Protectrice de la France, Contemple le Tiers Etat
figuré par un Laboureur poussant sa Charrue dans un Sillon. De la Ceinture de ce Cétoyen s'élevent des branches de Palmiers de
Lauriers, de Roses et d'Epis de Bled, Simboles de l'abondance; d'ou sortent des Têtes d'Evêques, Moines, Cardinaux, Militaires, et gens
de Robe. La Verité sortant d'un Nuage tient dans ses mains une Tête Couronnée &c

1

2

HONNI SOIT QUI MAL Y VOIT.

3

VOEUX DU TIERS-ETAT. / 2 line captions under each of four rectangular compartments: [top left] NOBLE CITOYEN, *Protégez-nous* [top right] VERTUEUX PRéLAT, *Priez pour nous.* [bottom left] MINISTRE DU TRéPAS, *Epargnez-nous.* [bottom right] SOLDAT DE LA PATRIE, *Deffendez-nous.* [below] *Et nous vous nourrirons tous.* Etching, hand coloured; Pl. 17, 3 x 23, 6; size of compartments: 6, 5 x 8, 8 ; Wtmk Unsigned, undated [1789]

4

Untitled / one line / or two line captions under each of four compartments: [top left] *Des Barrieres Delivrez nous Seigneur* [top right] *Des Capitaineries et Gardes de chasses Delivrez nous Seigneur.* [bottom left] *De la Milice Delivrez nous Seigneur* [bottom right] *Des Suppots de la Chicanne Delivrez nous Seigneur.* Etching, hand coloured; Pl. 17, 3 x 23, 6; size of compartments: 6, 5 x 8, 8; Wtmk [JOUVENEAU A VERVIN 178?] Unsigned, undated [1789]

These two prints dating from the meeting of the Estates General in May 1789 incorporate in four compartments miniature reproductions of Rue Saint Jacques *imagerie*. The format is that of reproduction sets used by *marchands d'estampes* to show current series: One single plate may show up to sixteen square or rectangular compartments or up to eighteen medalions. During the Revolution the trade issued sets advertising caricatures (cf Bib. Nat. M99003 and Bib. Ars 220 no 163). The miniatures were usually arranged by themes (costumes, fables etc.) and could be bought for cut-outs (see Basset's and Lenoir's sets, Bib. Nat. Li 8). The two prints in the Chester Beatty Library show how within this format traditional *imagerie* could be used to convey a political message by forming a sequence of selected miniatures linked by appropriate captions. The first print uses designs from costume prints (of almanack or *Cabinet des Modes* type), with captions in the form of deprecations to the protectors of the third estate, parodying litanies of saint. At the third figure, the caption breaks into imprecation against finance ministers (an allusion to Brienne?). The second print is a set of vignettes on the life of the peasantry forming a loose narrative on encounters with the law. *Octroi*, gamekeeper, militia, clerk of courts all represent abuses frequently denounced in *Cahiers de doléances*. The caption is in the form of supplication as in the prayers said on Rogation days before Ascension Sunday.

VOEUX DU TIERS-ETAT.

Noble Citoyen.

Protégez-nous.

Vertueux Prélat.

Priez pour nous.

Ministre du Trepas.

Épargnez-nous.

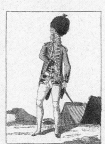

Soldat de la Patrie.

Deffendez-nous.

Et nous vous nourrirons tous.

3

Des Barrieres Delivrez nous Seigneur

Des Capitaineries et Gardes de Chasses
Delivrez nous Seigneur

De la Milice Delivrez nous Seigneur

Des Suppots de la Chicanne
Delivrez nous Seigneur

4

Untitled / Caption: four verse on two lines [left] *Pourquoi vous desoler l'un et l'autre en ce jour / c'est a vous doucement de sonner la retraite/* [right] *N en doutes plus amis la Sanction est faite / Et comme en la Chanson chacun a son tour*
Lettering in centre of design *Le Paysan Goguenard*
Etching, hand coloured; Pl. 20, 7 x 13, 1;
Des. 20 x 12, 3;
Wtmk [Fleur-de lys]
Unsigned, undated [October 1789]

The cartoon refers to the King's reluctant decision to sanction of the decrees of August 1789 which abolished the feudal rights of *privilegiés*. Louis first refused to do so, then signed some of them with reservations, and finally gave his unconditional sanction to the decrees and to the Declaration of Human Rights on 5 October. The cartoon celebrates the occasion with some bantering, calling on *privilegiés* to accept the new situation. The group featured is made up of a country man (a well-off *fermier* or *laboureur*), an aristocratic lady who appears near fainting and a distressed *abbé de cour*. The composition evokes a stage performance. Compare the design with no 10 (*Le Sort mérité*). In both cartoons, the centre character in a group of three strikes the dominant tone, and interaction between the three is dramatised by a theatrical lay-out.

LE JEU DE QUILLES. / *Je pars Monsieur l'Abé, j'ai manqué mon coup — Pour moi je ne le manque pas.*
Etching, hand coloured; Pl. 20, 1 x 13, 9;
Des. unruled;
Wtmk [J fleur-de-lys BERGER]
Unsigned, undated [summer 1789]

This delicately drawn and carefully coloured etching makes a subtle point about the new political situation after the Estates-General had declared themselves a Constituant assembly. The young noble in officer uniform has failed to score and is leaving the game (a hint of early emigration, as an idiom with 'quilles' means to take one's leave). The player at the game represents the Third Estate, whose turn it is to bowl; but the dialogue staged in the caption shows the clever player "l abatteur de quilles" to be the abbé, confident that he will score – an allusion to the prominent role played in the summer of 1789 by 'patriot' clerics, in particular perhaps by Abbé Sieyès. Skittles was a popular game, played by all and there is no intended derision in using it as a theme. A counter-revolutionary cartoon issued by Webert in 1792 uses the same motif to represent the international situation.

Le Paysan Goguenard

Pourquoi vous êtes-ôter l'un et l'autre en ce jour
C'est à vous doucement de sonner la retraite

N'en doutés plus *** la Sanction est faite
Et comme en la Chanson, chacun à son tour.

5

6

LE JEU DE QUILLES.

Je pars Monsieur l'Abé, j'ai manqué mon coup

Pour moi je ne le manque pas.

Untitled / *au voleur à l'assassin ou les acapareurs d'argent.*
Lettering [bottom left hand corner]:
assignation Contrat viager
Etching, hand coloured; Pl. 25,7 x 22,1;
Des. 22,9 x 17,3
Unsigned, undated [July-August 1789]

This print addresses a rural audience, though the central design and particularly the poses, gestures and costume of the three central characters evokes a theatrical performance. The title-owner and the lawyer take away the proceeds of their legal extortions protected by the marshlsea, whilst a group of peasants armed with swords, a stick and a scythe rush to the attack. This arousing print combines the grotesque representation of stock characters (the crested helmet of the *maréchaussée* is a standard part of a roman costume for the stage) with a realistic representation of the peasantry standing up for themselves – a significantly new image of a peasants' rising, which breaks away from the traditional representation of rural rebellious as hordes of savages. The design makes excellent use of the line of the mound and of the church in the background to add depth to the scene. A "Great Fear" spread through many regions during the month of July 1789 fuelled by rumours of hoarders and brigands. This print testifies to the fact that visual propaganda had a part to play in the anti-feudal revolts which occurred during that period.

Untitled / *Pas plus loin Messieurs, vous avez assez Volé. Pour toi Pauvre Hypocrate, il ni a ni Cri, ni regrêt, il faut que tu y passe.*
Etching, hand coloured; Pl. 26, 2 x 18, 4;
Des. unruled; Wtmk
Unsigned, undated [August 1789]

A satirical allegory on the long debates which followed the adoption in principle of the abolition of feudal rights and privileges on 4 August 1789. Exclusive gaming rights were quickly abolished (without compensation), but the question of tithes (made complex by enfeoffment) led to heated debates. In this cartoon the 'patriot huntsman' free now to shoot as he pleases, has already bagged a seigneur, and takes aim at clergy, whose 'turn has come'. The visual conceit of adding wings to human figures dressed so as to denote their social position is not particularly successful. The idea comes from the two meanings of the verb 'voler' (to steal, and also to fly) as the caption shows; but the plucked seigneur on the ground looks like an elegant fallen Icarus and the clerical fowl in the air, like a dressed up angel. Postures of all characters are conventional and appeared inspired by model designs.

7

8

Le Chasseur Patriote

L'or plus loin Messieurs vous avés asséz Volé. Pour toi Pauvre Hypocrate il n'a ni Crimi regrét, il faut que tu y passe.

*au voleur au voleur à l'assassin
ou les acapareurs d'argent.*

9

Untitled / *Saute Marquis ... et toi Hipocrite* Lettering on shop sign : *A la buvette du Tiers Etat*.
Etching, hand-coloured; Pl. 27,4 x 21,4;
Des. 24,6 x 18,2
Unsigned, undated [1789]

———

This scene combines two traditional visual themes which in 1789 become vehicles for populist ideology - the tavern ("la buvette du Tiers-Etat") and the street show (with trained dogs, representing the aristocracy and the clergy). Two cartoons also dating from 1789 show a man and a woman drinking and proclaim "J'sommes du Tiers Etat" (DV 2023 and 2024). Keeping the *privilégiés* up on their toes is also a familiar theme of revolutionary propaganda. The red cap as a symbol of liberty was used in the United Provinces in the 17th century, and was already quite common in 1789, though it only became a vogue in 1791 when it complemented sans-culotte dress. The attractive and sophisticated design, despite its apparent simplicity has unfortunately been partly spoiled in this print by an intemperate use of black by the *gouachier* (the person employed by the print publisher to colour etchings).

10

Untitled / no caption /
Lettering in centre of design: *Le Sort merité*.
Etching, hand coloured; Pl. 24, 3 x 18, 7;
Des. unruled
Unsigned, undated [1789]

———

The cartoon dramatizes the message of the Revolution as it is received by a young peasant, an aristocrat and a character who seems to represent a lawyer (note the curious headgear in the foreground). The papers (posters or newssheets) prominently displayed spell out the consequences for each: the young peasant points to liberty; recoiling in horror the aristocratic landlord and his agent (?) receive dire warnings of prison and death. The cartoon catches the mood of rebellion against seigneurial rights which swept part of the country during the summer of 1789. Movement is conveyed by postures; heads and arms denote reactions. The composition uses the central figure to bring equilibrium between the two animated figures on each side.

Le Sort merité

9

10

Saute Marquis ... et toi Hipocrite

11

Untitled [Marie Antoinette as chimera]
Lettering [in medalion circle] *Mme * * *
Laspict.* [on sheet held by chimera]
*Drots de l homme Constitution des fren-
cais*
Aquatint in grey; Pl. 11, 3 x 15, 3; Des.
[outer ring] 7, 7 [inner ring] 6, 6 diam.
Unsigned [Villeneuve], undated [Au-
tumn- Winter 1789]

12

Untitled [Marie Antoinette as hyena]
Aquatint in grey; Pl. 10, 3 x 13, 8; Des.
[outer ring] 7, 7 [inner ring] 6, 6 diam.;
Wtmk [FIN T DUPUY Heywood no
3301-04]
Unsigned [Villeneuve], undated
{Autumn-Winter 1789]

13

Untitled [Louis XVI as pig with horns]
Aquatint in grey; Pl. 12, 8 x 17, 9; Des.
[outer ring] 7, 7 [inner ring] 6, 6 diam.
Unsigned, undated [Autumn-Winter
1789]

14

Untitled [Comte de Provence as cat]
Lettering (in medalion circle] *M^r * * * le
Chat.*
Aquatint in grey; Pl. 10, 8 x 15, 8; Des.
[outer ring] 7, 7 [inner ring] 6, 6 diam.;
Wtmk {FIN T DUPUY Heywood no
3301-04]
Unsigned [Villeneuve], undated [Au-
tumn- Winter 1789]

This set of four animal cartoons satiris-
ing Marie Antoinette, Louis XVI and his
brother Comte de Provence, are attributed to Villeneuve by Bruel and show his
characteristic fine line and tone. Composite pictures such as these originate in
the medieval tradition of monsters, demons and marvels, the iconography of
which was made popular in the early
Renaissance by woodcuts illustrating
legendaries or imaginary voyages.
In this the traditional typology of monsters, hybrids of man and animal are
one category amongst others: most hy-
brid monsters are a mixture of several
kingdoms, genres and species, and hy-
pertrophied or atrophied human shapes
are at least as frequent. Apart from the
classical centaurs, animals with human
heads are usually representative of Sa-
tan (see Dante's Inferno Canto XVII),
though images of pigs with human
heads feature in the 1557 edition of
Lycosthenes's *Chronicon* and in woodcuts illustrating Odoric and Mandeville.
Later on Chimeras and Hydras become
popular satirical devices and the late
eighteenth century favours the traditional figure of a man with an ass's head
(the emblem of stupidity, as in Messmer
prints) or anthropomorphic designs.
Villeneuve in grafting a face profile in
the true likeness of an individual upon
an animal body, renews the iconology
of prodigies but with a satirical intention, starting a trend in animal caricatures of the Royal family which is particularly favoured by prints in the popular
manner. His first design, Marie Antoinette
as a chimera, is derived from a series of
prints *à la harpye* which appear between 1784 and 1788. The conceit was
inspired by a pamphlet published in
1784 and purporting to describe a "symbolical monster" found near Santa-Fe,
and written under a transparent pseudo-
nym by Louis Stanislas Xavier, Comte de
Provence, the brother of the King
whose title was "Monsieur" (*Description
historique d'un monstre symbolique...
par Francisco Xaveiro de Meunrios*, Paris 1784). Villeneuve's design is greatly
simplified. His monster is shown tearing
with its claws a piece of paper on
which is inscribed 'Rights of man' and
'Constitution of the French'. The inscription in the medalion identifies it as an
"*aspit*", i.e. the fabulous animal of medieval Christian iconography which is the
emblem of covetousness, greed etc.
With the *pendants*, Villeneuve moves
towards greater realism in his animal
representation (note in particular the
excellence of the cat arching his back);
though he adds small symbolic details
to the heads of Marie Antoinette (snakes
for ringlets) and to that of Louis (the
horns, the sign of the cuckold – cf.
O'Neale's representation in his frontispiece to the 1765 edition of George Ste-
ven's *A lecture on heads*). The animals
are chosen for their traditional characteristics: the hyena for its meanness and
viciousness, the pig for its gluttony. The
latest and most topical emblem of the
four is that of Monsieur, brother of the
King, shown as a cat, representing devi-
ousness. Monsieur, Comte de Provence
was involved in a plot by an officer of
his Guard, Marquis de Favras, to remove
the King from Paris, and allegedly to as-
sassinate La Fayette. Favras was arrested
on 24 December 1789, tried and hanged
on 19 February 1790, having revealed
nothing.

Mme*** L'aspic?.

11

M*** le Chat.

14

13

12

15*

Untitled / *Le niveau National*
Key to main characters [from right to left]
1 Il êst trop gros et trop gras à l'Egalité il Consent. 2 le Niveau est Nécessaire.
3 J'ai peur de me perdre sans l'Aise par l'Egalité, que deviendrons nous. 4 Jadis nous etions Gentils et maintenant nous voila Vilains.
Etching, hand coloured; Pl. 31,9 x 25,6; Des. 28,3 x 20,6
Unsigned [M.A. Croisier], undated [1789]

This well known revolutionary print has been attributed to Marie Anne Croisier. The treatment of faces shows similarities with "l Apothicaire de Grenoble" (no 39) and with "Leçon donnée par Robespierre" (no 65*). The imaginative treatment of arm movements gives animation to the line-up of twelve characters, representing the new process of national levelling and renovation. Surveying and construction devices are prominent, and the building metaphor links the two aspects of equality and reconstruction. At the centre, given prominence by blank spaces is a national guard using a water level and taking his bearings from his two colleagues on the left; on the right is a derrick, a mechanical contrivance used to slide building blocks into place. Mechanical devices are often used in prints to represent the new political processes. Here the building metaphor links the two aspects of social equality and national renovation, in an image of equalitarianism which avoids abstraction and allegorization. A touch of matter of fact joviality is introduced by the figure of the aristocrat [Philippe-Egalité?] in his red coat who has to be strapped into place, and by the figure of the fourth national guard at the back ready to do some further trimming with his sword, if needs be.

16

Untitled / A LA BONNE HEURE ... CHACUN SON ÉCOT ...
Lettering [below bust of Louis] *Au Regenerateur de la France.* [on paper held by Marie Antoinette] *Le clergé renonce a ces privileges pecuniaires*
Etching, hand coloured; Pl. 28,9 x 21,9; Des. 24,2 x 15,6
Unsigned, undated [late summer 1789]

A late 18th century *joie de vivre*, celebrated by many artists in the 1770's still pervades this elegant print issued in the summer of 1789. The discreet political message is delicately handled : note the bust of Louis XVI with the title of "Regenerateur de la France" in its cartouche well integrated into the decoration, and the figure of Marie Antoinette tastefully dressed in the new national colours, talking to her customer. He is a well dressed bourgeois in a relaxed pose, representing the Third Estate. Seated at a pedestal table and finishing a game of chess are an aristocrat in officer's dress and a member of the clergy. The title of the cartoon expresses the relief felt by the Tiers, now that "everyone is paying his fair share". Harmony restored is the message also conveyed by the airy composition, the sophisticated architectural perspective, the delicate colours. The finely drawn detail adds to the impression of good taste. The interior represented is that of the *Café de Foy* in the Palais Royal.

A la bonne heure ... Chacun son écot ...

17

Untitled / [in large cartouche] *Premier hommage des Habitans de Paris à la Famille Royale le mercredi 7 Octobre 1789. lendemain de son heureuse arrivée dans cette Ville [verse] Famille Auguste et tendre avec transport cherie / Lorsque nous voyons parmi nous réunie / Que vous puissiez rester dans nos murs desormais / C'est le voeu le plus doux de tous vos vrais Sujets*
Etching, hand coloured; Pl. 13, 9 x 20, 7; Des. 12, 4 x 13, 8; Wtmk [star]
Unsigned, undated [October 1789]

Commemorative prints celebrating events in the life of the Royal family are an established genre before the Revolution; they are often commissioned by the crown as a means of propaganda. Elaborate line engravings were copied by *imagiers* for popular distribution. Revolutionary printmakers often use in derision themes from Ancien Régime official propaganda. This print, dating from the early days of the Revolution, deliberately breaks away from the high art allegorical or historical manner to present a new image of the Royals in the fashionable new genre of family portraiture. The arrangement of the group places the Royal children between their parents at the centre, creating a happy image of a united *notables* family. The discreet but elegant curtaining forms a canopy framing the group, apparently snapped as they would appear to their people, at a Palace window or in a first tier box at the theatre. Behind the group, the figure of Madame Elisabeth (?) the children's governess wearing a fashionable blue bonnet, and the faces of two footmen discreetly glancing at the scene, add a touch of informality and spontaneity to the occasion.

18

Untitled / no caption
lettering: *Cette fois ci, la justice est du côté du plus fort.*
Etching, hand coloured; Pl. 24, 4 x 19, 7; Des. unruled; Wtmk [grapes]
Signed AP., undated {1789}

An early use of the device of the seesaw by the author of a number of "patriot" cartoons (who signs himself AP.). An impression of lightness and playfulness is achieved by the absence of background, and by the long oval base upon which the seesaw appears to be 'mounted'. Noble, abbé and national guard sit on the plank like children at play. In contrast note the resolute posture of the woman representing justice, shown facing the viewer, her right foot firmly settled on the plank which bends under her push.

19

Untitled / in lieu of caption an inscription in the centre of the design: *Sur les Frontieres de Luxembourg au poste appelé de ce nom, Gardé par une sentinelle Française de notre côté, de l'autre par une de lEmpereur. Notre sentinelle fit remarquer la Cocarde Nationale de son Chapeau a la Sentinelle Allemande, qui aussitot main sur son coeur et renversant son fusil la crosse en haut, fit connoitre ses intentions amicales envers une Nation libre.*
Etching, hand coloured
Wtmk [jar with fleur-de-lys]
Unsigned, undated [late 1789?]

A political parable designed to raise morale and boost the confidence of a patriotic audience in the peaceful triumph of revolutionary ideals. The inscription carefully placed at the centre of the picture tells the story and draws its moral. Illustration is kept to the essential: the Austrian guard (from the Luxemburg fortress) acknowledges the new national colours worn by the French guard, a soldier from the regular regiments stationed at Nancy (the gate of the fortress, featured in other cartoons is shown on the right-hand side). The bridge over the Moselle prominent under the inscription becomes a symbol of peace and friendship.

Premier hommage des Habitans de Paris à la Famille Royale
le mercredi 7 Octobre 1789 lendemain de son heureuse arrivée dans cette Ville.
Famille Auguste et tendre avec transport cherie,
Lorsque nous vous voyons parmi nous réunie.
Que vous puissiez rester dans nos murs desormais,
C'est le vœu le plus doux de tous vos vrais Sujets.

Cette fois ci, la justice est du côté du plus fort.

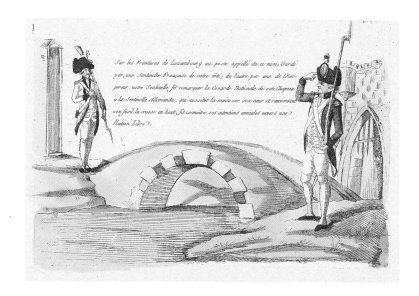

Sur les Frontières de Luxembourg au poste appellé de ce nom, Gardé par une Sentinelle Française de notre côté, de l'autre par une de l'Empereur, notre Sentinelle fit remarquer la Cocarde Nationale de son Chapeau à la Sentinelle Allemande, qui aussitôt la main sur son cœur et renversant son fusil la crosse en haut, fit connoître ses intentions amicales envers une Nation Libre.

20

Untitled / *A beau mentir qui vient de loin*
Etching, hand coloured; Pl. 20, 4 x 16, 4;
Des. 18, 1 x 13, 7
Wtmk [? Serpent]
Unsigned, undated [? 1789]

21

Untitled / *La Graine de Niais*
Etching, hand coloured; Pl. 26, 7 x 17, 6;
Des. 24, 8 x 14, 4; Wtmk
Unsigned, undated [? 1790]

These two illustrations of proverbial sayings are not directed at identified targets, but comment on "the times that we live in". They warn that people should not believe all that is being said. Animal characters stage a little fable to illustrate the point. Turkeys feature prominently in the cartoonist *ménagerie*. The 'dindon' can represent blindness combined with pretentiousness, as in one of Florian's fables which popularised the original type. Politically, as in *Générosité revue et corrigée*, the dindon represents, as Marat himself put it, one of those 'patriots without vertu, full of self esteem...'. More often a flock of "dindons" represents the gullible, particularly those who blindly believe what priests tell them, as in *Nouvelle Synagogue de l'Ancien Curé de Saint-Sulpice* (Blum no 268). The first of these cartoons illustrates this theme: the preacher is a fox in capuchin habit, a motif which goes back to the medieval period. The composition echoes that of a well known satire inspired by Florian on the subject of Calonne addressing the notables in 1787 (*Le Singe Cuisinier*). The literal meaning of the phrase "venir de loin" (= from far away lands) has given to the cartoonist the idea of locating his apologue in a modern exotic setting, with wild birds. He has created an image evocative of illustrated "Voyages" and "Descriptions", taking advantage of the recent vogue of such works or of novels

such as *Paul et Virginie* (1788). The parrot perched on the branch fits in with the décor, and reinforces the point. The second cartoon is also in the format of book illustrations, in its case books of fables, tales or proverbs, though etched on a larger scale. In keeping with the Rue Saint Jacques manner, the design is reduced to the essential: a rural setting on the edge of a wood (a folktale location) and realistically drawn animals. The wolf enticing his prey is an old exemplum (found in Aesop), but the central place assigned to the sack of wheat full to the brim and the inclusion of a windmill on the hill in the background, would strike a deep echo in collective mentalités. 1790 was a good harvest year; does the cartoon warn that the wolves are nevertheless lying in wait?

A beau mentir qui vient de loin

La Graine de Niais.

Untitled / *Voila ce que c'est que de les avoir trop longs.*
Etching, hand coloured; Pl. 20, 9 x 15;
Des. 17, 3 x 12, 1
Unsigned, undated [1790]

———

A comment on the suppression of *corporate* privileges, illustrating the literal translation of the French idiom "Rogner les ongles" (to clip someone's claws). There are a number of cartoons on the same theme, with variations in the characters represented and in the captions. As is often the case for cartoons using the body or parts of the body as their satirical device, this one combines 'before', 'during' and 'after' stages. Note that the character awaiting his turn wears the long robes of a president of a Parlement Court.

Untitled / *Messieurs Delaunoy Flexelles Berthier Foulon et les deux Gardes du Corps qui ont été Decolés par le Peuple, voudroient passer jusqu'aux Champs Elisées en dépit de Caron qui ne recoit dans sa barque que le Sr Remy François Boulanger Victime innocente de la Fureur Aristocratique: l'infortuné Calas et autres vienne le recevoir a l'autre bord.*
Etching and dry point, hand coloured;
Pl. 21, 3 x 16, 8;
Des. 20, 2 x 13, 9; Reg. mks
Wtmk [Posthorn]
Unsigned, undated [1789-90]

———

The political intention is clear and effectively expressed by the theme of Charon the ferryman, which was familiar to both popular and educated audiences. The murder by a mob of Remy François, a baker wrongly accused of cheating on quality was exploited by counter-revolutionary propaganda, as an example of mindless revolutionary violence. An engraving was published commemorating the King's gift to the baker's widow. In this cartoon, of the victims of early revolutionary justice, only the innocent Remy François is taken on board the ferry which travels to the Elysean fields, where Calas and other victims of Ancien Régime arbitrary justice prepare to receive him. The cartoon does not gloss over violence in its use of the emblematic image of severed heads on sticks. The caption though attributes to 'aristocratic fury' the murder of the unfortunate baker; and the contrast between the elongated headless silhouettes used for the group on the left, and the near pastoral scene on the right, leaves no doubt as to where sympathies should go. Balance is achieved in the composition by the centre group with its use of reversed symmetry for the postures of the ferryman and his passenger. A satirical 'dialogue of the dead' *Les Enragés aux Enfers* about the same events may have provided the cartoonist with his idea. The theme is also used in a con

temporary cartoon warning Aristocrats of their fate *(Avis aux Aristocrates)* and later by Villeneuve for his *Reception de Louis Capet aux Enfers* (1793).

Voila ce que c'est que de les avoir trop longs.

23

22

Messieurs Delaunay Flexelles Berthier Foulon et les deux Gardes du Corps qui ont été Decolés par le Peuple, voudraient passer jusqu'aux Champs Elisées en depit de Caron qui ne recoit dans sa barque que le Sr Remy François Boulanger Victime innocente de la Fureur Aristocratique. l'infortuné Calas et autres viennent le recevoir a l'autre bord.

Untitled / *Le Joli Moine Profitant de l'occasion*
Etching, hand coloured; Pl. 26, 7 x 21, 8; Des. 24, 6 x 18, 5; Wtmk [grapes? Heywood no 2424]
Unsigned [Basset], undated [1790]

This witty and lively print is both a trade advertisement in the traditional manner of Rue Saint-Jacques print makers and a topical scene which comments on the secularisation of religious orders in the good-natured spirit of popular anti-clerical satire. The scene is set at the corner of Rue Saint-Jacques and Les Mathurins, where Basset's shop was situated. The shop is shown in the background, with hand-coloured prints displayed on its front. The half-open door gives a glimpse of the interior with a shop girl seated at a counter. A street pedlar leaves the shop carrying on his back a basket filled with his purchases. The inscription on the side, is from the caption of a popular print on the three estates ("il faut esperer que ce jeu finira bientot"). Basset's shop sign is prominently displayed over the door. Under the trade mark the inscription "*Magazin de Mauvaise Copie ou il s'entrouve quelque fois de bonne*" is an in-joke: Basset Père was sued for pirating Esnaut and Rapilly' plates of Modes et Costumes français in 1779. On the right hand side, a wig maker cum barber's shop. Its sign proclaims "*Ici on secularise proprement*" (secularisations neatly performed). Through its open door can be seen a monk being fitted with a new wig. The group in the foreground performs a short comical sketch: a tailor brings a new hat and a pair of breeches to a monk about to be defrocked; a young girl sitting on his knee prepares to shave off his beard, but even before the change can take place, the monk eagerly "grabs the opportunity" (note the position of his left arm). The *topos* (beard and head shaving) is an old one, already found in Dutch republican prints of the seven-

teenth century. During the Revolution it is mainly associated, as in this print, with the theme of the secularisation of the clergy. Here it is treated comically rather than seriously, with a touch of bawdiness which stays within the register of the traditional jokes told by the populace about their clergy. Nevertheless in its association of the two themes of trade and politics, this print illustrates a new perception of the role of printed images brought about by the Revolution, and also testifies to the commercial sense of print makers responding quickly to the openings thus created.

Untitled / *l'Erreur et la Folie nous avoit jetté dans les Cloîtres mais la raison nous rend au monde.*
Etching, hand coloured; Pl. 26, 9 x 16, 8; Des. 23, 5 x 12, 6 [traces of other lines,? result of separate impression of caption]; blue paper; Wtmk [? Fleur-de-lys]
Unsigned, undated [Spring 1790]

The cartoon celebrates in a light vein the interdiction of monastic vows and the suppression of most religious orders (13 February 1790). It is in the manner of *badinage* etchings: the clergy have replaced the nymphs and satyrs, but the setting (a park, statues in perspective) is a salute to Fragonard's *fantaisies*.

l'Erreur et la Folie nous avoit jetté dans des Cloîtres mais la raison nous rend au monde.

Depart du General parisien pour la fameuse nuit du 5 au 6 octobre / mes amis menez moi je vous prie a Versailles
Aquatint in sepia; Pl. 8, 7 x 11, 8;
Medal. 7, 3
Unsigned, undated, [1790].

1790 has been called 'the year of La Fayette'. Building on his early popularity and his prestige as commanding officer of the newly formed 'National Guard', La Fayette saw himself as able to control the people of Paris and as the benevolent protector of the constitutional monarchy. His role during the October days of 1789 was presented as an instance of his capacity for leadership. This royalist cartoon (note the inn sign with the name Ludovi[c[us]] in the background) jeers at this self-proclaimed image, and at the role of protection aassigned to the *Garde nationale* (see no 93*). Eyewitness accounts confirm that the 'Paris general' had less than total control of the mixed mob of guards and armed rioters who caught up with the crowd of women after they had marched on Versailles on October 5th. It was late in the day (the clock in the cartoon shows 10.35) when La Fayette rushed to Versailles, and as the cartoon plainly indicates he was led rather than leading. In this composite street-scene the street lamp (*la lanterne*) is a reminder of mob rule. La Fayette appears in his satirical persona as man-horse.

PRO PATRIA VINCERE AUT MORI DÉDIÉ A LA NATION / *J.B. Cretaine agé de 60 ans quoi qu'ayant eu le poignet droit entierement meurtri à la Bascule du 1er Pont de la Bastille se releva, fut devant le grand Pont des Tours, ou l'epée nue à la main il somma par 3 fois. l'ennemi de se rendre. La lame de son epee fut cassée d'une balle, un homme fut tué a ses côtés et malgré ses blessures il fut assez heureux de prendre le Major, le fit son Prisonnier le remit a 2 Gardes Françaises entre les deux Ponts. Ce 14 Juillet. 1789.*
Etching, hand coloured; Pl. 13, 5 x 22;
Des. 13, 5 x 16, 8; Wtmk
Unsigned, undated [Summer 1790]

Prints celebrating civic or military heroes have a long history; they originate in particular in the United Provinces during the Sixteenth-Century where woodcuts celebrate popular heroes, and engravings military and civic leaders. Their importance for civic and patriotic propaganda was understood by the French monarchy which encouraged their production during the latter part of Louis XVI's reign. Their format combines a representation of the hero at a telling point of the action with an explanation in the form of a narrative. They were designed as exemplars of outstanding courage or military virtue, and as rewards for those thus honoured with popular fame. In the latter part of the Eighteenth Century, a new emphasis began to be put on morality and virtue: a 1776 print issued by d'Orléans and other provincial printmakers honours a *Rosière*, a local girl awarded a prize for virtuous living. This print is in the more traditional military genre and uses the conventional representation of soldiers returning from battle. It commemorates the 'vainqueurs de la Bastille' publicly feted in 1790. J.B. Cretaine must be the older character on the left, though the focus is on the upright fresh faced hero shown on the right. In prints of this kind, the image is not always in harmony with the narrative: here this is a source of some ambiguity

as the broken sword which should be carried by Cretaine is shown in the younger man's hand – the scene could thus appear to describe Cretaine capturing the Guards' officer. The point of the representation is primarily to extol courage and comradeship as patriotic virtues, and to instil in all a sense of duty. The Latin motto used as title is adapted from Horace's third Ode. It appears to be the motto adopted by the Batalion of Veteran Volunteers which was being formed as part of the Paris Guard in 1790 (it is featured on a later Almanack of the Batalion). The idea of a Veterans' batalion was met with sarcasm, and a number of pamphlets were published deriding it. This print may also be a form of reply to these reactions. Citizen Cretaine was one of the 954 who were awarded the title "Vainqueur de la Bastille" in June 1790. His true age was seventy-two. He was a bourgeois (i.e. a *rentier*) and had lost two sons in the American War of Independence. He was therefore an appropriate respectable figure to propose as an example of courage worthy of comradeship, and as an illustration that age is no obstacle to valour.

Depart du Général parisien
pour la fameuse nuit du 5 au 6 Octobre

Mes amis menez moi je vous prie Coucher
à Versaille

PRO PATRIA VINCERE AUT MORI   DÉDIÉ A LA NATION

J.B. Crosaine agé de 60 ans quoi qu'ayant eu le poignet droit entièrement
meurtri à la Bascule du 1er Pont de la Bastille se releva, fut devant le grand
Pont des Tours, ou l'epée nue à la main il Somma par 3 fois, l'ennemi de se rendre la
lame de son epée fut cassée d'une balle, un homme fut tué a ses côtés et malgré
ses blessures il fut assez heureux de prendre le Major, le fit son Prisonnier
le remit a 2 Gardes Françaises entre les deux Ponts
Ce 14 Juillet 1789

28

Untitled / *Patience Monseigneur votre tour viendra*
Etching, hand coloured; Pl. 25, 3 x 17, 9; Des. 24, 7 x 14, 8; Wtmk
Unsigned, undated [early 1790]

A well known cartoon inspired by the decision of the National Assembly of 2 November 1789 to appropriate Church property. In December a first lot of land was impounded and put on sale, though legal difficulties hampered the process. The first lands to go were those owned by monastic orders (suppressed in February), though sales of other property could not go ahead until funds were assigned to the upkeep of the secular clergy. The cartoon shows a monk and an *abbé* having already disgorged their gold, whilst a fat bishop waits for his turn to come. The contraption, in the centre, is a wool scourer, a device used to squeeze wool before carding. The cartoon gleefully associates realistic imagery and grotesque representation for wide popular appeal: as in other cartoons, the tool or implement (e.g. a carpenter's level) is used to express the political process (the 'treatment') whilst body deformity symbolises either political, social or moral taintedness. In this and other cartoons also, contrast between a 'before' and 'after' stage (an old satirical device) emphazises the desired result. The success of this composition can be gauged by the number of variants of this cartoon which were issued with additional lettering.

29

Untitled / *Helas je ne peut vous donné puisque l'on m a tout oté.*
Lettering on design: Assemblée Nationale
Etching, hand coloured; Pl. 21, 5 x 15, 6 ; Des. 17, 9 x 12, 7
Unsigned, undated [1790]

A theatrical cartoon staging a dialogue between a citizen and a priest: the background is in the manner of a stage set. Set attitudes and gestures belong to conventional depictions of alms giving scenes. The representation of the *Manège* where the Assembly met is idealised; wooden barriers and awning were in place, but in the design they are arranged to create perspective, and to suggest perhaps both covered paddock and playhouse (two former uses of the *Manège*). The cartoon comments ironically on the despoiling of the Clergy.

Patience Monseigneur votre tour viendra

Helas je ne peut vous donné puisque lon ma tout oté

Untitled / [verse on 4 lines] *Illustres deffenseurs, ferme appui de nos Loix. D'immortelles couronnes sont dues a vos exploits, Vous avez abbatus cet Hydre redoutable. Le fleau de la France; ô Hommes incomparables!*
Etching, hand coloured; Pl. 17, 1 x 15, 1; Des. 15, 8 x 11, 1
Unsigned, undated [1790]

This cartoon praises the record of *Parlements* as defenders of the Catholic religion. The counsellors sit in their black robes: on one of two versions, the ecclesiastical counsellor is distinguished by use of purple. The président wears red. The apparition represents the Church with its traditional attributes (cross and chalice). The cartoonist may have wished to appeal the superior courts to come to the defense of traditional church rights by reproducing this rather conventional representation. In September 1790, the Parlement of Paris did try to invalidate a decision of the Paris municipality on a case related to church property; but feeble attempts by counsellors to resist the new legal order were doomed. The courts were abolished on 5 October.

Untitled / *Le Restaurateur Embarassé*
Etching, hand coloured; Pl. 21, 3 x 14, 7; Des. 20 x 10, 9; Wtmk
Unsigned, undated [1790]

The title "Restaurateur de la liberté française" was given to Louis XVI by the Assembly on 11 August 1789. The obvious double-entendre provided the cartoonist with the idea of the cartoon. The fact that restaurants were a new phenomenon added piquant to the representation. The cartoon shows men in uniform entering a monumental kitchen and discovering a group busy cooking a meal. The room is bare and there is an element of surprise and embarrassment suggested by the gestures of the group at the door, the posture, the raised arm, the turned head of the figure holding the frying pan. On the stool on the left-hand side in the foreground, the sheet of paper bears the inscription "Compte-rendu", an allusion to Necker's first published budget of 1781: These first public accounts revealed the huge pensions which privilégiés received from the Crown (the clergy is shown here, blowing on the fire with bellows, whilst the nobility, denoted by the crested helmet, pours wine into the pan). The cartoon could be an allusion to the recall of Necker by the King under pressure of the Assembly on 16 July 1789. But, given its title, it is more likely to reflect Necker's growing unpopularity in 1790, when he was suspected of "faire la cuisine", i.e. to use his past reputation to make palatable to the public a defense of the monarchy and of hereditary privilege. Whatever its political intention, this etching would have delighted connaisseurs for its lightness of touch, the life-like quality of its sketching, in a composition which makes excellent use of space, thanks to the classical quality of the architectural framing.

Illustres deffenseurs, ferme appui de nos Loix,
D'immortelles couronnes sont dues à vos exploits,
Vous avez abbatus cet Hydre redoutable.
Le fleau de la France, ô Hommes incomparables!

Le Restaurateur Embarassé

32

Untitled / *l'Abbé Verd Dansant une Bourrée avec la soeur Rose au son de Moine-au ou la Soiree du Ranelack*
Etching, hand coloured; Pl. 21, 9 x 16, 1; Des. unruled
Unsigned, undated [Spring 1790]

This cartoon is the work of a brilliant artist, schooled in the tradition of Italian cartoonists, but familiar also with the earlier style of Saint Aubin. The artist combines an ability to render movements by lively contours and to bring life to attitudes by dislocating bodies, with an effective use of space and an economy of design in the best rue Saint Jacques manner. The theme of clergy frolics is an old one, but was given a new topicality when in February 1790 the Assembly forbade monastic vows and suppressed religious orders. Several cartoons of the same period show the clergy enjoying their newly found freedom: There are *Rendez-vous* in Bois de Boulogne and *Soirées* in Palais Royal (see Blum nos 172 and 174). This one is located in *Le Ranelach*, an entertainment park opened in imitation of Chelsea at La Muette in 1774. Soon fashionable it was frequented by court ladies: note the young novice, in the background of the cartoon, attempting, fan in hand, to deport herself like a lady of fashion. The centre group shows an *abbé* and a nun dancing to the sound of a serpent (a rustic instrument, and a symbol of temptation) played by a monk seated on a stool. The step is that of *bourrée*, though the hold is more like that of *allemande*. The *bourrée*, a country dance, had become fashionable, but the cartoon stresses its rustic origins (stool, serpent, ruddy complexions). The dancers are shown enjoying themselves but not with the gracefulness or flair of court dancers: Note the exaggerated movements of the *abbé*, the coy awkward expression of the nun about to do a turn. A key hangs from her belt, a reminder of her still recent release.

The caption gives silly nicknames to the characters based on harmless (and not very good) puns. Derogatory puns on the word *abbé* feature in the captions of a number of later more aggressive cartoons against non-juring clergy. See those described in DV 3405-3414, and nos 42 and 35* (*Ah! pendard* and *Combat entre le Pere Duchesne et l'Abbe Caissè*) probably by the same artist.

33

Untitled / *Je vous l'avoit bien dit Mr l'Abbé qui falloit mieux ployer que de rompre.*[On the pyramidal tomb, left hand side] I*ci repose ce grand corps qui mangeoit les Vivants et les Morts.*
Etching, hand coloured; Pl. 21, 7 x 15, 7; Des. 17 x 12
Wtmk [JOU.. A VERVIN]
Unsigned, undated [1790]

A citizen extends his sympathy to an abbé, telling him "I told you so; better bend than break". This is a scene of mock mourning: on a bier are laid out ecclesiastical vestments, a bishop's hat and crozier, an aspersorium. Behind it is a pyramid with the inscription "here lieth that great *Corps* which ate up the living and the dead". The theme of the clergy's funeral, is used in a number of satirical pieces and cartoons: cf. the pamphlet *Grand Messede Requiem... pour son Altesse serenissime Monseigneur le Clergé de France..* (Tourneux no 15537) and the two cartoons showing the Clergy's funeral *cortège* (DV 3042, 3043); a fertile visual theme originally applied to privilégiés, it was later turned around and used against *Clergé Constitutionel.* The occasion of this cartoon is the vote by the Assembly on 13 April 1790, rejecting a proposal to declare the Catholic religion the national religion. In April the Assembly prepared to dispose of all ecclesiastical properties and

discussed the related issue of the funding of public worship. In the heat of the debate, members of the High Clergy (Dom Gerle and the Archbishop of Aix), sermonized the Assembly and defended the establishment of the Church and the corporate identity of the Clergy, thus ensuring by intemperate speeches, the defeat of their cause. The cartoon draws the lesson, in a fairly savage comment and in a laconic style. Note though that the *abbé* has lost his biretta but still retains his calotte.

l'Abbé Verd Dansant une Bourée avec la Sœur Rose au son de Moine-au ou la
Soirée du Ranelach.

Ici repose
ce grand corps
qui mangeoit
les Vivants
et les Morts.

Je vous l'avoit bien dit Mr. l'Abbé qui falloit
mieux ployer que de rompre.

34

Untitled / *La Culbute*
Etching, hand coloured; Pl. 20, 8 x 26, 8;
Des. 18, 5 x 22, 7; Wtmk [Strasburg Lily]
Unsigned [by the author of *l Abbé Verd?*], undated [1790]

"Au bout du fossé la culbute" is a proverb applied to those who persist in their errors and go for a fall. Here a fat abbot falls into a ditch to the great delight of two country folk (note the clogs). This masterful composition makes full and economical use of the space provided and of the denoting contrast between black and bright colouring, making the figures 'jump' out against the blank background. Movement is conveyed by an organizing structure of lines formed by the arms and legs of the falling figure, repeated in those of the broken fragments of the stick. A counterpoint of hand-movements and exaggerated facial expressions immediately convey the feelings of the participants. Caricature, comic of situation and comic of expectation all contribute to the delight that the spectator would take at watching a representative of clerical opulence finally come a cropper. The graphic style of this print is highly personal and unmistakably belongs to the creator of the pugilist *Père Duchesne*.

35*

Untitled / *Combat entre le Pere Duchêne et l'Abbé Caisse. Le Coup de Poing.*
Etching, hand coloured; Pl. 19, 9 x 26, 8;
Des. 18 x 22, 3;
Wtmk [wreath with large fleur-de-lys]
Unsigned [by the author of *l Abbé Vert?*], undated [1790]

The two pugilists form an image which is perfectly inscribed inside the frame of the picture. The bent elbow of the figure on the right together with the outline of the slope and the edge of the frame delimit a blank space which brings out the jagged edge made by the clothes of the falling body, rendered more striking by the generous use of black gouache. Apart from the small trees which evoke distance and bring out the dip of the mound, the only added detail is the black calotte which flies away punctuating the movement of the head. The group is inscribed inside a narrow base trapeze which squashes the lower part of the bodies to concentrate the representation of the action in the torsoes, arms and fists of the pugilists. The cartoonist has taken great care to emphasize the muscular arms and the broad chest of Pere Duchesne and the billowing shirts, by modelling them with fine etched lines. There is evidence of *retroussage*. Similar treatment gives life and vivaciousness to the profiles. As in *vues d'optique* depth is provided by a mound coloured in green and a blue hand for sky. With his own Pere Duchesne the artist has created a unique image. Its source is not the pipe smoking figure of the newspaper, but an archetypal figure, common to both which like the soldier *La Tulipe* belongs to the legendary of *Ancien Régime* popular urban culture. The graphic motif may be inspired by a distant engraving by Romeyn de Hooge for N. Petters' celebrated handbook on self defence (published in Amsterdam in 1674) or by more recent English boxing prints.

The two pugilists though are not prize-fighters: they are men of the street who have got into their shirts' sleeves. This Pere Duchesne is settling old accounts, in a manner which captures the vision that urban folk liked to have of themselves, strong, impetuous and slightly mischievious (note the red tongue which Pere Duchesne sticks out at his adversary). The brisk graphic style is similar to that of *L'Abbé Verd* (no 32); so is the punning caption. The use of a mound as a setting, the expressive contrast of bright colouring against black, the technique used for modelling also show in *La Culbute*. All three cartoons are probably by the same skilled artist.

La Culbute ?

Il ne sçait sur quel pied Danser. / Danse Aristocrate
Etching, hand coloured; Pl. 31, 1 x 22, 8;
Des. unruled; grey paper;
Wtmk [? foolscap]
Unsigned, undated [late 1790]

The balancing act of the tight rope walker made familiar by circus acts, fairs and street shows is a device with broad comic appeal used by both left wing and right wing satirists (cf *Garre au faux pas*), to represent the tricky game of politics. A common idiom is applied literally and figuratively to the position in which Abbé Maury (immediately identifiable in the print) found himself, once the King had sanctioned on 23 July 1790, the decree organising the Constitutional church and requiring the Clergy to take an oath of allegiance to the Constitution. Maury was out on a limb: he had to abandon his earlier uncompromising rejection of the *Constitution Civile*, and adopt a new line of defense based upon the rights of the Gallican church. Despite this and the publication of an *Exposition des principes sur la Constitution civile du Clergé* by 30 bishops, on 26 November, the Assembly imposed the requirement of taking the oath of allegiance within eight days. In this print which is often misinterpreted, the artist has placed at the centre of the image under the tight rope, a figure dressed in Arlequin clothes but with a Pierrot ruff and devil wings. The intention is not simply to add to the street show atmosphere. The gestures – one hand shaking the rope, the other rubbing soap on it, and the forked tongue denote that Maury is about to 'trip' over his own slippery words – hence the various postures of mock encouragement, surprise or shock displayed by the spectators on each side.

Untitled / *Pour avoir passé les bornes il s'est cassé le Nez*
Lettering: *Que le Diable te ramasse*
Etching, hand coloured;
Unsigned [produced by Basset?],
undated [1790, April?]

An *abbé* stumbles against a corner stone whilst running and falls to the ground. The cartoon tells this little story by compressing the narrative into its climatic moment when the *abbé* is caught by the devil as he falls. Two visual details serve as conventional representations of the cause (the huge corner stone) and the effect (the nose bleed). They are visual metonymies, translating into visual terms the literal meaning of two idiomatic phrases which, in their figurative sense are used in the caption which provides the explanation: The *abbé* went too far (*il a passé les bornes*) and has come a cropper (*il s'est cassé le nez*). The young peasant on the right comments on the action in words and gesture, like the *gracioso* of Spanish comedy. The words he speaks are inscribed beside him ("let the devil etc"...); the raised palms turned towards the spectator are a common gesture expressing lack of care or concern. The elongated figure of an ecclesiastic moving away from the pillar stone explains the occasion and provides the political context. It belongs to a revolutionary grotesque, the 'defatted' cleric, featured in Basset's anti-clerical production. The house style of this cartoon, and the mode of composition (by an assemblage of copied designs) suggest that it also originated from Basset's shop. Though a true likeness was not attempted for the profile of the impetuous *abbé*, the long nose, the grey wig and particularly the floating short cloak (worn by abbés de cour) were sufficient to denote Abbé Maury to a public familiar with this style of production. Maury was the target of a number of other cartoons (also attributed to Basset) which are all variations on

the theme of Maury and the Devil: cf DV 2002 and 2003, and the pamphlet *L'Abbé Maury aux Enfers* drawing on the same inspiration. Maury was the tempestuous defender of the Clergy's corporate rights in the Assembly, and became notorious in 1790, for a number of episodes during which he clashed with other *députés* (including Mirabeau) or had to be removed from the speaker's podium. In April 1790 he was censured by the Assembly. In November he was involved in a brawl with other deputies and complained of being lampooned in broadsheets sold by street hawkers. The caption of this cartoon makes it clear that it refers to a specific incident probably the censure motion.

Il ne sçait sur quel pied Danser.

Danse Aristocrate.

Que le Diable te ramasse

Pour avoir passé les bornes il s'est Cassé le Nez

38*

Assemblee des Capucins. / l Assemblée des Aristocrates, ou l'Harmonica des Aristocruches
Etching and dry point; Pl. 30, 3 x 15, 8; Des. 27 x 12, 3; Wtmk [JOU... AUV...]
Unsigned, undated [April 1790].

This masterly cartoon uses a simple idea – a visual pun, as its motif for an allegorical composition which both ridicules a particular event and 'debunks' its political significance. The event to which it refers is the protest meeting held on 12 April 1790 by a majority of députés of the high Clergy, after the rejection by the Assembly of a proposal made by Dom Gerle, a chartreux and député of the clergy of Riom, that catholicism should be declared the national religion. The meeting convened by Dom Gerle (shown in the centre of the picture) was held in the Church of the *Capucins*, and it issued a solemn declaration, without effect. The motif used in the cartoon (a 'cruche', i.e. a jug) is a trope for stupidity, a visual rendering of a common idiom ("bête comme une cruche" = as stupid as can be). The jugs are arranged in a semi-circular design around the figure of Dom Gerle. A speaker's podium on the right and a chair and desk on the left denote the meeting; the jugs in the proximity of Dom Gerle are arranged like the humming glasses of a harmonica, suggesting some kind of harmony produced by their hollow vibration in response to his bell. The scene is set against an architectural decor which represents the actual *Capucins* location. The linear perspective selected is that of architectural views. The contrast between its straight lines and angular shapes — stonework, pillars, drapes — and the rounded shapes of the jugs is arresting. It creates an eerie feeling of overpowering stillness reinforced by the ground angle view: the spectator looks in on the scene as if upon an archeological cache placed inside a basement, or in a crypt. Details reinforce this atmosphere: a basket (holed) in the foreground; a rat just escaped from a trap crawling along the basement edge; an owl sitting still, perched on the head of the statue-like figure of Dom Gerle, bags (of wheat?) lying on the steps. The cartoonist succeeds in conveying an impression of deadness, whilst avoiding monotony and retaining a sense of humour. He varies the shapes of the jugs; there are tumblers, pitchers, urns (even a chamber pot); some are with cordons and crosses. Two stand out from the lot: the tumbler on the president's chair splashing some liquid upon the Assembly *arrêté*, and the jug on the podium dressed up like a preacher. The strange gathering has begun to produce some kind of sound under the magic wand whimsically appearing from behind the drapes. The message of the allegory is clear: the clergy are the derelict and vacuous remains of a bygone 'first estate'. Their final awakening is an illusion and their protest an echo from the tomb of the past. The visual motif was used later by David for one of his caricatures against the English, commissioned by the Comte de Salut Public (*L'Armée des cruches*, 1794), but not as successfully.

39

Untitled / *L'Aristocrate Charlatan.* [Below] *Un Alchimiste que l'on dit etre un deserteur Fabrique a Grenoble et fait distribuer comme Journal cet Elexir sous l Etiquette le sens commun. Nous avons recu une topette de cette liqueur venemeuse et nous avons trouve par l'analise que le dit éléxir n'est qu'une preparation de Mercure distillé avec l'acide anti national et a dissoudre la Constitution notre Alchimiste ne scait donc pas que ce sont la des montagnes de Grenouille inattaquables aux yeux Aristochimiques! Vu l'etiquette du dit Eléxir.*
Etching, hand coloured; Pl. 24, 4 x 14, 7; Des. 19, 8 x 11, 7
Wtmk [Peloux?]
Unsigned, undated [1790]

The satirical device of showing leading figures in the world of politics and public opinion as quacks selling their panaceas to the gullible has a long pedigree. This "alchimiste de Grenoble" and his elixir recall the celebrated "charlatan espagnol" and his catholicon from the 16th century *Satyre Menippeé*. The same analogy is used between speech or discourse and quack medicine. In this cartoon the design is copied from satirical representations of Law's banking establishment in rue Quincampoix during the Regency (note the monkey, the hunchback, the attitudes of the public, the woman reading at the foot of the stand). The treatment of faces shows some influence from English cartoons. The caption is couched in the language of Faculty pronouncements, with the inevitable play upon the word *Mercure*, the title of the quasi official newspaper which reported assembly debates. Parodies of this kind, associating proprietary medicines and journalistic productions are not uncommon in pro-revolutionary cartoons (e.g. *L'Onguent national,* against *Actes des Apôtres*). This one attacks a publication called "*Le Sens commun*". Only one copy of a single number of this periodical is known to exist. Its editor is satirised in the cartoon as a charlatan from Grenoble who holds anticonstitutional, pro-aristocratic views. He could only be Mounier, leader of the so-called 'monarchiens', who resigned from the Assembly after the October days and returned to his native town, from which he emigrated to Switzerland later in 1790.

L'Aristocrate Charlatan.

Un Alchimiste que l'on dit etre un deserteur Fabrique a Grenoble et fait distribuer comme Journal cet Elexir sous l'Etiquette le sens commun.
Nous avons recu une topette de cette liqueur veneneuse et nous avons trouvé par l'analise que le dit elexir n'est qu'une preparation de Mercure
doublé avec l'acide anti national et a dissoudre la Constitution notre Alchimiste ne scait donc pas que se sont la des montagnes de Grenouille
innattaquables aux yeux Aristochimiques! Vu l'etiquette du dit Eléxir.

Untitled / no caption / inscriptions over characters, [left] *Carosse et Chevaux à vendre* [centre] *Ils sont passés ces jours de Fête* [below female on the right] *Je t'en ratisse*
Etching, hand coloured; Pl. 21, 6 x 16, 7;
Des. 19, 5 x 14
Unsigned, undated [1791]

The coach, a symbol of state, then a trope for the unity of the nation, features in this cartoon as the sign of the changed fortunes of *privilégiés*. The luxurious carriage (note the suspension, an English or Dutch improvement of recent date) is for sale, so is the horse which is being led away. The postures show the coachman humbly waiting for a parting tip, the old abbé (with walking stick) and the young lady, back from their *promenade*, turn him away. Servants were hit hard by the ailing fortunes of *privilégiés*, and by emigration and often found themselves out of work as a result. Social satire is given a political edge in the cartoon by the words ascribed to the *privilégiés*, and by the denoting position of their arms and hands. The abbé searches his front pocket, and apologetically mutters that the halcyon days are gone; yet gold coins escape from the purse which he holds. The young lady uses a vulgar phrase of the time ("*je t'en ratisse*") which indicates a promise made to be broken, punctuating it by a characteristic dismissive gesture.

Les Gros ont toujours mangé les Petits le temps passé n'est plus. / Comme tous les Monstres ont des Reptils qui les avertissent de leurs mortels ennemis De meme les Aristocrates ont les petits Maitres pour Moniteurs.
Etching, hand coloured; Pl. 29, 1 x 19, 7;
Des. 26, 1 x 16, 5;
Wtmk [wreath with small fleur-de-lys]
Unsigned, undated [1791?]

As snakes warn crocodiles of deadly danger, so do young dandies with aristocrats. The cartoon illustrates the analogy by representing within a single design, framed by its sea shore setting two images belonging to separate graphic traditions distinct in topic and in manner, but intended as two representations of the same moral. One, in the style of cheap illustrations of wonders of the natural world, shows the Nile crocodile warned by the snake that his legendary enemy the ichneumon, the Egyptian rat, is about to attack it. The other, could, on its own, be a piece of social satire on fashion, influence and money, treated à la Rowlandson. The artist has attempted to introduce some visual correspondances between the two, the snake-like hand of the dandy, the gaping mouths of crocodile and aristocrat. Politics makes its appearance on the left-hand side, with the group of national guards. Its place in the composition provides a point of reference common to both representations, but does not quite succeed in overcoming the oddity of their juxtaposition. The title is equally puzzling for it also juxtaposes two proverbial phrases ("big fish eat little fish" and "times have changed"), neither of which is illustrated by the design. Revolutionary cartoons were fond of recycling proverbs, and Gautier noted in his *Journal de la Cour et de la Ville* of 20.6.91 "that everything is changed, even proverbs". It may be that this is one of the lessons that the cartoonist intended here. The word *Moniteurs* used in the caption, evokes the name of the quasi official newspaper which reported debates in the Assembly. Could the open purse and the gold coins hint that its journalists were in the pay of the aristocratic party?

Carosse et Chevaux à Vendre.

Ils sont passés ces jours de Fête

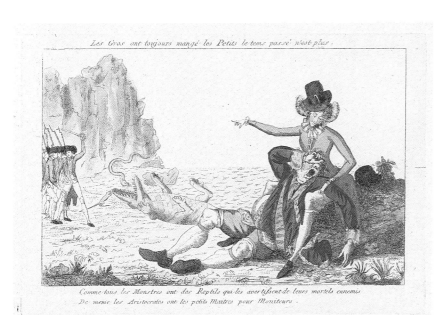

Les Gros ont toujours mangé les Petits le tems passé n'est plus.

Comme tous les Monstres ont des Reptils qui les avertissent de leurs mortels ennemis
De meme les Aristocrates ont les petits Maitres pour Moniteurs.

42

Untitled / *Ah Pendard tu veut avoir la femme et encor la bourse. Combat d'Arlequin avec le Reverend Pere Dom Assinon.*
Etching, hand coloured; Pl. 21,8 x 25,1; Des. 19 x 20,8; Wtmk [...AUVERGNE]
Unsigned , undated [1791]

A number of cartoons use as their satirical device characters and scenes from Boulevard and Foire theatres (between which companies alternated). Acrobatic acts, dance shows and *parades*, are often chosen to represent politics, italian comedy and puppet shows to satirize the Clergy's position. The satirical imagery in this cartoon comes from one of the numerous Arlequinades performed by these companies in the years 1790-1793, at the *Gaieté, Variétés Amusantes* or *Vaudeville* playhouses. Arlequin is the epitome of Comedia dell-Arte theatre extremely popular before and during this period. The fact that the character riding behind him looks like a travesti Pierrot, and that actors' feet are shown under the pantomime horse and donkey suggests that an actual performance is represented here, and that Dom Asinom, the third character named in the caption, may be featured in an actual play. The encounter depicted is adapted from a set piece (a "constrasto"), with a specific target in mind made clear in the caption: the regular clergy, having first taken the people's money, now want to take their women. This is an apparently harmless piece of anti-clerical fun, using an old cliché. Attitudes of ordinary people towards secularised clergy were often ambiguous: supporters of the suppression of monastic orders, and of a 'Constitutional' church resented the behaviour of some secularised monks and many objected to the idea of married priests. Tensions were heightened by the Pope's Brief of March 1791 and peasant and artisan opinion, until then united on religious issues began to be split. This cartoon seeks to exploit the situation and is an example of propaganda aiming to stir up feelings and fuel agitation.

43

Untitled / *Polichinelle vainqueur des Aristocrates. Ah ah c'est aussi un Aristocrate. Eh bien porte cela en ta Chapelle*
Etching, hand coloured; Pl. 18, 3 x 24, 7; Des. 17 x 22; Wtmk
Unsigned, undated [1791]

This cartoon also borrows its satirical character and its representation from the popular stage. Polichinelle is used in satires published during La Fronde and also features in Molière's plays. This one however comes straight from puppet shows, of the type given at the Saint Laurent and Saint Ovide's fairs. His image is standard: two humps, a crooked nose, a stick. So is the episode, a variation on one of three set situations, Polichinelle and the authorities. The character on the ground is dressed in the conventional Spanish costume of stage aristocrats (a reference to Beaumarchais's Count Almaviva?). The action (depicted by contrasting parallel and angular lines in the position of arms and legs) is a set piece: Polichinelle gives a good drubbing to those by whom he appeared, or pretended to be fooled. It's the moment of reckoning: the priest too is an aristocrat in disguise. Compared to Arlequin, Polichinelle has lost some of his vitality on the late eighteenth-century stage, but he remains an attractive figure, providing a useful persona for a representation of the People (note the clogs): quarrelsome and insolent, jovial and above all shrewd, he has brought down the aristocracy and is about to expose the clergy.

Ah Pendard tu veut avoir la femme et encor la bourse.
Combat d'Arlequin avec le Reverend Pere Dom Assinon.

Polichinelle vainqueur des Aristocrates.
Ah ah c'est aussi un Aristocrate. Eh bien porte cela a ta Chapelle.

Untitled / *Saint pierre Renient le Pape pie VI*
lettering on cartoon: *paradie*
Etching, hand coloured; Pl. 17, 4 x 25, 9;
Des. 15, 2 x 21, 6; Wtmk [M]
Unsigned, undated [April 1791]

The Papal Brief condemning the Civil Constitution of the Clergy (10 March 1791, but only published in extenso in *L'Ami du Roi* of 4 April) gave rise to a number of prints. This one shows Saint Peter denying Pious VI access to Paradise, a theme illustrated by at least two others (DV 3460, 3463). The Pope's condemnation had major consequences for the clergy, and its impact on popular opinion was made all the more vivid by a ceremonial burning of a dummy of the Pope which took place in the *Palais Egalité* on 6 April . The occasion offered an opportunity for cartoonists to recycle much traditional iconography and to resurrect old themes. Some come from the sometimes obscene anticlerical sub-literature of the period (cf. *Lettre du Diable au Pape*, 1790, Martin and Walter no 8776). Others take the opportunity to parody familiar religious genre scenes (e.g. visions or apparitions, as in the aquatint *Tu n'as point imité l'exemple des apôtres*). Most of those in the popular manner recycle conventional representations of clerics and devils. They show no awareness of another tradition, that of German Reformation woodcuts with their sweeping displays of grotesque monsters, and are more likely to be inspired by satirical engravings against the Jesuits or by the more recent etchings against Mesmerism. This cartoon like others on the same theme is a montage of designs. The group of St Peter and companions denouncing the Pope, and the general composition may be an echo (reversed) of Rafael's famous *Christ's charge to St Peter*. The kneeling posture of the Pope holding his Brief, comes from the general iconography of visionaries and apparitions.

The demon who holds him by the throat is lifted from an etching against Mesmer, *Le Mesmerisme à Tous les Diables* (circa 1784). A whimsical touch is introduced by the rustic cockrel perched over the door to paradise, an allusion to St Peter's Denial, but also an allegory of national vigilance.

Untitled / *Naissance des Aristocrates / le Lavement a produit son effet au Diable le fumet*
Etching, hand coloured; Pl. 17, 8 x 24, 7;
Des. 17, 2 x 21, 3;
Wtmk [JO... A... ? ON]
Unsigned, undated [1791]

The cartoon belongs to a number of anti-clerical ones inspired by reactions to the Pope's Brief *Quod Aliquantum* (of 10 March, but known in France only in April). After it was known, many bishops retracted their oath of allegiance. The Papal Brief, comments the cartoon, has had the desired effect of an enema, expelling the 'aristocrats' from amongst the High Clergy (note the medical clyster in the foreground). The central devil figure is a set piece, used to place others around –a motif and composition of medieval origin. The cartoon is a collage of common designs and traditional images by different hands. The devil figure (14, 7 high) is out of proportion, and the whole design just fits in the size of the plate.

Untitled / *Lancée et Vomissé St. Pere tout ce que vous avés de plus noir dans l'esprit, invoquée les Demons pour qu'ils vous inspire tout ce qu'il y a de plus affreux, imité vos infame disciples qui se sont couvert de tout les crimes les plus execrables et vous r'empliré par cela votre St. Ministere, Mais la Nation Françoise craint peu vos foudres, et malgré toute*

votre malignité elle fera revivre, cherir et respecter cette Ste. Religion que vos Satelites avoit avilie par la Cupidité et leurs infames débauche. Lettering: *Eveques et Archeveque excommunié / Vicaire et autres Pretres excommunié / Assemblée Nationale excommunié*
Etching, hand coloured; Pl. 27, 9 x 18, 8;
Des. 26, 5 x 15, 7; Wtmk [FIN DUPUY Heywood no 3302-04]
Unsigned, undated [April 1791]

Of the satirical prints which attack the publication of the Papal Brief condemning the new *Constitution Civile du Clergé*, this one is the most violent. The idea comes from the burning of the Pope in effigy at the Palais-Royal organised by the satirical journalist Gorsas (who edited Courrier de Paris) on 6 April 1791. Burning a contumax in effigy was part of the panoply of Ancien Régime punishments which were abolished by the Assembly. The event took place in Palais-Royal, a centre of journalistic, publishing and print-making activity. Gorsas's parodic execution was essentially a farce in poor taste played upon his right wing competitors. As shown by a print illustrating no 73 of Desmoulins's *Révolutions de France et de Brabant*, Gorsas also burnt copies of Royou's *L'Ami du Roi* (where the Brief had been published) as well as *Journal de la Cour et de la Ville*, and *Actes des Apôtres*. The event though caught the imagination of patriots and anti-clericals, so much so that it is represented in the major collection of *Tableaux historiques de la Révolution Française* (Plate no 51 by Prieur and Berthault). This cartoon makes no concession to humour or irony: the rather comical devils which feature in others on the same theme are absent (compare with DV 3465). Anticlerical verve in the popular manner usually draws upon stock imagery inspired by distant Reformation prints or recent anti-Jesuit satires. Here there is a conscious attempt at visual and verbal violence: note the

44

Saint pierre Reniant le Pape pie VI

45

Naissance des Aristocrates
Le Lavement a produit son effet au Diable le Fumet.

powerful image of flames and smoke, the reds and yellows of the fire echoing those of the Pope's vestments. The imagery is close to scenes of public burnings illustrating sixteenth and seventeenth-century martyrologies, or to eighteenth-century representations of auto-da-fes: the dominant colour, yellow, evokes that of the san-benito worn by some of the condemned, the Pope's tiara resembles their bonnet. He is shown in distress vomiting his excommunications, barefooted, with the flames already licking his left sole. The figure of the imploring helpless bigot on the right adds to the dramatic impact. The cartoon is intended not to amuse but to arouse anger and its caption is couched in highly vituperative language. Prints dealing with the Papal Brief, like those on the *Constitution Civile du Clergé*, can be formed into a loose narrative sequence, though styles differ. In its treatment of flames, in the choice of denoting colours, and in the style and hand writing of the caption, this print resembles *Arrivée du Pape aux Enfers* (DV 3464), whilst n 44 is closer to DV 3465.

47

Untitled / *Vive la Liberté – Vive la Liberté*
Etching, hand coloured; Pl. 14, 4 x 17, 9;
Des. 12, 5 x 15, 1
Unsigned, undated [? 1791]

This dramatic figure of a prisoner in chains uttering a celebrated cry provides an emotional allegory for the abuses of arbitrary rule and for the longing for freedom. The image immediately evoked is that of the Bastille and of its tales of forgotten prisoners. Landelle (?) published an aquatint on the discovery of a skeleton during its demolition (Carnavalet 1977 no 339). The design though is not realistic; the setting is that of the *souterrain*, a stock set for early

Gothic plays just becoming fashionable on the stage at the beginning of the Revolution. Mrs Radcliffe was first published in French in 1791. The *Opera Comique* gave performances of *Camille ou le Souterrain* by Dalayrac in 1791. The décor in the print looks like the wings which made it possible for spectators to watch what was taking place beyond centre stage. The format is that of book frontispieces. The hypnotic quality of the composition is achieved by the stress put on the double arch which encircles the picture and closes in upon the figure of the prisoner, by the repeated motifs of bars and by the darkened lunette. A single glimmer of hope is provided by a hardly distinguishable oil lamp hanging from the ceiling. This dungeon is imagined as much as real. Together, the chains, the arch, the bars, and the steps for ever out of reach, are also an evocation of the phantasms latent in the collective psyche of the times. The composition recalls representations of St Paul in his gaol but without the conventional jug of water; and the design is very similar to a celebrated "Liberty" print (with the motto "Vry heid, bly heid") from A. Spinneker's Supplement to *Leerzame Zinnebelder* (Harlem, 1758).

48

Untitled / LEGISLATEUR FUTUR [below, verse on two lines] *Et souvent tel y vient qui sait pour tout secret, / Cinq et quatre faut neuf otez deux, reste sept Boileau Sat. 3* [below, 6 line verse, on 3 columns, begins] *Depuis deux ans venir en France Vous y brillés par la depense* [ends] *Vous dicterez la loi nouvelle Car un marc d'Argent vous valez* [chorus] *Ah vous en serez bis / Il est certain que vous en serez. Que vous en serez.*
Lettering inside border around medalion: *Toi meme repond moi dans le Siecle ou : nous sommes Est ce au Poids savoir qu on mesure. les Hommes*

Lettering [on head band:] *1 Marc* [on purse:] *act/ions/ de la caisse*
Etching, hand coloured; Pl. 13, 4 x 20, 1;
Des. 12, 3 x 12, 3
Wtmk [Posthorn with bell]; Reg. mks
Unsigned, undated [June 1791]

This portrait of the law maker of the future associates human elements and objects intended to be read as signs of wealth. A measure with an ornate handle is used to represent the head, to signify that wealth does not mean brains. The theme is one which is often illustrated in the Dutch satirical prints collected under the title *The Great Mirror of Folly (Het Grote Tafereel ... 1720)*, where the scroll frame borders of some engravings also mix curved metal shapes with human faces. The quote from Boileau's *Satire*, used in the caption, makes the same point. The cartoon refers to a clause for the new Constitution adopted in October 1789. A property qualification was introduced for candidates to the new Assembly: candidates had to show they paid tax equivalent to one *marc* d'argent (the marc was both a measure and a weight used for bullion). Few députés opposed the clause at the time, but protest gradually spread amongst *sociétés populaires*, and on June 15 1791 the clubs presented a petition to the Assembly. This cartoon is most likely to have been produced during this period. The figure of the *Legislateur futur* is featured on at least one other cartoon of the same period. (Bibl. Nat. Coll. Hennin 10484).

47

LEGISLATEUR FUTUR

Et souvent tel y vient qui sait pour tout secret.
Cinq et quatre font neuf otez deux, reste sept. Boileau Sat. 8.

48

Vive la Liberté-Vive la Liberté

49

Untitled / *La toupie d'Allmagne*
Etching, hand coloured; Pl. 13, 2 x 20, 3;
Des. unruled
Unsigned, undated [Jan-March 1791]

Louis-Henri-Joseph de Bourbon, son of
Le petit Condé, leader of *émigré* nobles
recognised by his moustache is shown
enthralled by the noise of his huge
humming top; small in stature (by comparison with his great ancestor) he is
quashed by the disproportionate size of
the toy. A humming top is called in
French a 'toupie d'Allemagne'. The idea
conveyed is that Condé is kept amused
whilst the foreign powers and Leopold
in particular shun plans for armed intervention. By displacement the caption
also applies to Condé, who like a spinning top is the toy of foreign powers,
only capable of producing harmless
noises. In cartoons, toys (including toy
soldiers and yo-yos) are often associated with *émigrés* and the Condés, to lower them to the level of silly children; the
spinning top and child scene is an echo
of Chardin's *L'Enfant au Toton*.

La toupie d'Allemagne

Untitled / *Les Deux font la paire*
Etching, hand coloured. Pl. 23, 1 x 15, 9.
Design unruled (a proof?). Wtmk
Jug with fleur de lys (7 x 4, 5)
Unsigned, undated, May-July 1792.

The technique and style are those of
Rue Saint-Jacques productions. The appeal is popular: the familiar animal
trope, the pig a symbol of gluttony has
become politicised. Usually applied to
Louis (see nos 51* and 52) it stands here
for Marie Antoinette. The facile joke
porc-en-truie (pig in sow) is derived
from the name of Porentruy, a region
where French troops under Custine
scored the only success of the early
war, on 30 April 1792. Its visual expression required no explanation, and for its
caption an idiomatic phrase is used
which provides the additional comment
that King and the Queen are two of a
kind.
The King is depicted riding his mount.
The pose is that of formal equestrian
portraits. Decorations emphasize the
trappings (and the reins ...) of Royal office. The dress is cavalry and the sceptre is held like a lance. The posture of
the sow, head forward, ears pricked,
has a touch of the equine, but the teats
are definitely porcine. The group is set
on a slight mound which provides ele-
vation; the only detail a tree and a
shrub on each side on a different scale
gives a sense of perspective. Careful
use of white for the blank space and
off-white for the sow enhance the outline and the brilliant colours of the uniform.
The King's crown is detached from his
head and is falling to the ground. This
single depiction of movement calls for
the toppling of a monarchy whose dis-
credit in popular minds is made plain in
this grotesque portraiture.

Untitled / *ah le Maudit animal, il m'a
tant Pêné pour S'engraisser, il est si
Gras, qu il en en* [sic] *Ladre. Je reviens
du marché, je ne sais plus qu'en faire*
Etching and dry point, hand-coloured;
Reg. marks; Pl. 24, 4 x 17, 6;Des. 22,
6 x 17, 6
Unsigned, undated, [Summer 1791]

A number of cartoons appeared after
Varennes showing Louis as a pig. The
theme illustrated here is that of the
monarch as a useless social parasite: the
pig, as the caption informs us in direct
speech, is diseased - measled from too
much fattening. The fluid silhouetting of
the characters, the light touches of the
detail aim to give an impression of a
scene sketched from life. Note the revolutionary colours used for peasant's
clothes, and compare his cocky stance
and youthful complexion with the figure
in no. 52. The print also offers to its audience a new image of the peasantry
befitting its changing status and political
role.

Untitled / *Je me suis Ruiné pour
l'engraisser - la fin du compte je ne sait
pu en faire*
Etching, hand coloured; Pl. 22, 9 x 15, 9;
Des. unruled
Unsigned, undated, [Summer 1791]
Lettering: *l'entree franche*

A variation on the same political theme
as no. 51 , with the common motif of
the pig-King. The additional lettering refers to the suppression of all tolls by the
Assembly on May 1st 1791, and adds a
secondary theme to the main one. The
peasant is in traditional dress, though
the rosette commemmorates the newly
acquired freedom from trade barriers.
The face with its curly wig is curiously
similar to engraved profiles of the older
Voltaire.

l'entrée franche.

je me suis Ruiné pour l'engraisser — la fin du compte je ne sait pu en faire

Les Deux font la Paire.

53*

Untitled / *Retour de la Famille Royale, a Paris. le 25 juin 1791*
Etching, hand coloured; Pl. 36 x 26,5; Des. 34,2 x 23,3; Wtmk [letter C]
Unsigned, undated [july 1791]

This large print commemorates the return of the Royal Family under guard after their failed escape and their arrest at Varennes on 21 June. Having travelled with armed escort from Chalons, they arrived in Paris on the evening of 25 June. They were accompanied by three representatives of the Assembly, Barnave, Pétion and Latour Maubourg (shown here in yellow riding with the coach driver) and led by colonel Mathieu Dumas, shown in pink riding a light brown horse. The dramatic side view of the berline-coach with its diminutive passengers (only the Prince, the Princess Royal and Madame Elisabeth dare to look out) does not aim at a faithful representation of the arrival in Paris, as in reality, the national guards lined up the streets and had been ordered to reverse their arms. The print uses straight line composition and the repetitiveness of the soldier motif [fine lines of legs and bayonets, caps and blue coats] to create an eerie feeling which captures the mood of the return to Paris, where people stood and watched in total silence. To avoid monotony, the artist has introduced individual variations in the soldiers' faces. This successful print was copied several times, with new captions and the addition of a background of buildings and spectators which spoils the impact of the model (cf Carnavalet 1977 Nos 188 and 189).

54

Untitled / [on two cols] *Troc pour troc, Paris pour Montmédy, / Coeffure pour Couronne, Départ pour L'autriche* [below in fine lettering] *passport pour Mde De Caoffre du 21 juin*
Etching, hand coloured; Pl. 17, 1 x 24, 1; Des. 20 x 15; Reg. mks
Unsigned, undated [Summer 1791]

The cartoon imitates genre prints showing scenes of intimacy, made popular by genre artists such as Mallet and Boilly, but with a deliberate coarseness of treatment which is the opposite of their elegant affected manner. Louis is shown as a valet de chambre, with the grand cordon du Saint Esprit (but with a bottle stuck in his pocket), doing Marie Antoinette's hair, as they prepare to leave Paris for Montmédy. When arrested at Varennes, the Queen travelled with a false passport to the name of a Russian baroness, Madame de Korff (the de Caoffre of the caption). Louis was disguised as her valet. This pathetic charade is jeered by the cartoonist who deliberately debases the royal couple: (note the *bidet* featured in the bottom left hand corner), but not as crudely as some obscene prints showing Marie Antoinette gratifying her coiffeur.

55

Untitled / *Il est pris*.
Etching, hand coloured; Pl. 21, 3 x 14, 1; Des. 21, 3 x 12, 5
Unsigned, undated [late June 1791]

A satire on *émigré* reactions at the news that the King had been arrested at Varennes (note the prominent newssheet displayed in the centre). The composition stages a scene of pandemonium, in the lazzi tradition. The barrel in which Mirabeau Tonneau sits and which, with his legion cap, has become his emblem, features also in *Theatre Italien* routines. The reactions are denoted by postures and particularly by facial expressions: the long noses have become a conventional rendering of the French phrase 'faire un long nez' (to pull a long face). Amongst the characters are the bishop of Trèves and Mainz, where émigré nobles gathered, and perhaps on the extreme right and left the Princes.

56

Untitled / *Que faite vous la? Je suis en Penitence*.
Etching and dry point, hand coloured; Pl. 23, 8 x 16; Des. 21, 8 x 15, 4; on blue paper, Wtmk
Unsigned, undated [June 1791]

A number of cartoons use the theme of the King in a gilded cage, talking to a passer-by who asks him what he is doing there. The caption is in question and answer form. *Journal de la Cour et de la Ville* in its number for 18 June 1791 describes a cartoon where the questioner is the Emperor Leopold; the King answers "I sanction freely". This one shows a citizen asking the same question. The King answers that he is doing his penance.

Troc pour troc. Coeffure pour Couronne.
Paris pour Montmédy, Depart pour L'autriche.

passeport, pour Mrs Les Comte du 21 juin

Il est pris.

Que faite vous là : Je suis en Penitence.

57

Untitled / *he'hu! da da*
Etching, hand coloured, Pl. 22, 6 x 16;
Des. unruled; Wtmk [Crown with
Strasburg Lily]
Unsigned, undated [summer 1791]

The mount on the right and the clock
showing twelve noon spell out Montmédy
[Mont-midi]. The rebus refers to the
town near the border which the Royal
family were attempting to reach when
they were stopped at Varennes. This
cartoon derides the slow journey of the
Royals on their attempted escape, and
ridicules the King by representing him
like a child on a wooden horse playing
with a toy drum and crying "giddy-up!".
The bite of the satire is directed at
Marie-Antoinette and her relationship
with the King. She is shown as "the
power behind the throne" giving a push
to the simple minded Louis: Note that
the wooden horse has a tail made of
ostrich (= Autriche) plumes. Its head is
shaped like that of a stag whose horns
are sprouting – a traditional attribute of
cuckolds, and also a persistant reference
to slanderous rumours about "secret
orgies at Trianon", when as told by Soulavie, Marie Antoinette and her atten-
dants, having read in Buffon about the
mating of deer, dressed up as stags and
does and amused themselves "by playing out the love games of the deer".

58

Untitled / *J'en ferai un meilleur usage,
et je Sçaurai le conserver.*
Etching, hand coloured; Pl. 26, 9 x 19, 8;
Des. unruled; Wtmk [Crown with
Strasburg Lily].
Unsigned, undated [summer 1791]

This print also uses the device of representing the King as a child at play, to
deride his incapacity to govern after
Varennes. Louis is reduced to the
toddler's stage, playing with a toy windmill. Contrary to other satirical prints on
the same theme, this one also conveys a
precise political message. The young
boy in a fashionable sailor's outfit is the
Dauphin. He is shown taking away the
royal sceptre from the King's hand (despite Marie Antoinette's admonition)
and claiming, according to the caption,
that he would use it better and know
how to keep it. In the constitutional crisis created by the suspension of the
King after Varennes, there were some
who favoured placing the young Dauphin on the throne – a solution encouraged by Duc d'Orléans who would have
been appointed regent.

bé hu! da da!

J'en ferai un meilleur usage, et je sçaurai le conserver.

Untitled / *Le Pere Duchesne et Jean Bart. Duch. Qui est tu Sacre Dieu. Jean Bart: Aristocrate et je m'en fout.*
Etching, hand coloured; Pl. 18, 6 x 24, 9; Des. 16, 1 x 21, 7;
Wtmk [JOVENEAU AVIGNON[?] 1788]
Unsigned [? Henriquez], undated [early 1791]

There were several *Pere Duchesne* and several *Jean Bart*: these periodical publications (and the many pamphlets which take their cues from them) cultivated a highly coloured style in the popular register, combining political rhetoric and provocative swears which became their trade marks (see the caption). They mixed *exposé* with vituperation, making use of catchphrases in their titles which anticipate headlines used today by popular newspapers. The two major *Pere Duchesne* publications (Lemaire's and Hébert's) and some of the counterfeits used a woodcut which showed Pere Duchesne smoking a pipe. This helped to fix his image of a sans culotte *gouailleur* in the minds of an audience of artisans and soldiers, who often clubbed together to buy subscriptions. Jean Bart, the sailor was his most successful rival. A publication entitled *Jean Bart ou suite de Je m'en...*, appeared in Paris in a total of 181 numbers in 1790-91 (see Tourneux no 11641). From no 121 it had a vignette showing the two characters seated at a table smoking. The encounter represented in this cartoon uses the same general idea, but in a free flowing graphic style which brings life to the characters, and is much different from the coarse woodcut of *Pere Duchesne*. An artist's hommage to two imaginary characters which had become iconic images, the very incarnations of the Voice of the People? The first editor of Jean Bart was L.M. Henriquez, a member of a family of engravers of that name, and we suggest his name for a possible attribution.

Untitled / *Ils ne m'ont laissé que deux Chicots*
Aquatint and etching, hand coloured; Pl. 13, 9 x 20, 6; Des. 11, 9 x 18, 9
Unsigned, undated [1791]

As soon as the Estates General met, print editors launched a series of portraits of the *députés*, who could purchase copies to send to their electors. A number of such collections were thus produced by Feisinger, Vérité, Desjabins and Bonneville. This cartoon parodies the genre, applying it to a type, the non-juring clergy. The ageing ecclesiastic is shown in profile, mouth gaping with no teeth "except" as the caption complains "two stumps". The same caption and the same theme are used in a coloured etching, where the priest is shown full length leaning on a walking stick (DV 3073). The pulling of teeth is an old satirical topos, used in the revolutionary *repertoire* to represent the radical removing of entrenched privileges. The full length caricature is more aggressive in style than this cartoon. Here the pinched face, the raised eyes and supplicating expression elicit derisory sympathy rather than scorn. This in part is due to the parody of the portrait format which extends to the round frame and cartouche, the crosshatching and the imitation of stipple for background. Note also the decorative ribbons over the oval frame, in the manner of portraits published by Esnaut and Rapilly.

L'echasseur pigmee de wormes Envoié exstraordinare A Mr, refugié a Mons. / no caption
Etching, hand coloured; Pl. 21, 8 x 15, 1; Des. 21 x 15, 1
Unsigned, undated [Summer 1791]

Humour, comedy and political satire combine in this cartoon which draws upon a number of traditions. Funny couples contrasted by their sizes are part of a common comic lore. The Fat and the Thin are a topos often used in Dutch morality prints. The Gargantua-pigmy theme is applied in revolutionary cartoons to the gluttony of the monarchy. Here the slightly bloated figure represents Provence, brother of the King. Each figure is treated as a separate caricature, in contrasted rounded and angular styles capturing two different physiognomies. Their manner shows that the cartoonist is familiar with both English and Italian caricatures. The little man too small for his boots may in turn have influenced English satires on Napoleon. Here he represents le *Petit Condé*, leader of *émigré* nobles. Condé is sometimes shown on stilts (see Blum no 507 le *Va-t-en-voir du Petit Condé*): Note the equivocation in the title on "le chasseur"– "l'echasseur" (l'echassier = one who walks on stilts). Despite the contrasted styles of the caricatural figures, the print works as a single image. The composition is held together by the parallel lines joining to form two right angles: the sword and cordon of Provence, the rifle of Condé. The main link is provided by the stretched arm of Condé along the main diagonal which focuses attention on the letter with inscribed address depicted at the centre of the image. The point is to show Condé in the role of political courrier. Other cartoons also show him in the demeaning posture of a messenger boy – an obvious jeer given the fact that his name was at the time linked to sommations, manifestoes etc. This print dates from June 1791, when the Comte de Provence made his successful bid to leave France. Having reached Mons, Provence received news of the King's arrest at Varennes. The caption states that Condé comes from Worms, a point denoted by his Austrian uniform, complete with fancy ostrich (i.e. Autriche) feathers. He is shown having arrived post haste (note the step

Ils ne m'ont laisse que deux chicots

Le Pere Duchesne et Jean Bart.

Duch. Qui est tu Sacre Dieu. Jean Bart. Aristocrate et je m'en fout.

designed to convey movement). The message he delivers is from the Emperor, an allusion to Leopold's request that Provence should not proclaim himself regent despite the arrest of Louis at Varennes. The obvious implication is that Condé is nothing but a *chasseur* on the Austrian pay-roll.

62

Untitled / *The Frogs who wanted a King*
Lettering on flag: *Martial Law*
Etching and aquatint in dark sepia;
Pl. 24, 5 x 18, 5; Des. 23, 3 x 15, 6;
Wtmk [... DUPUY FIN cf Heywood no 3306 and 3307]
Unsigned, dated ["Published by Act of Parliament 14 July" in reality July 1791]

The theme comes from Aesop and was popularised by Nevelet and then by La Fontaine in Bk III of his *Fables* (Fable 4 *Les Grenouilles qui demandent un Roi*). The apologue of the frogs who replace their "Stick of a King" by a 'Crane' who gobbles them up, is often illustrated in editions of proverbs and fables. In at least one Dutch satirical print it is used, as in this print, to comment on politics. The dating and the caption in English used in this cartoon are obviously spurious. A key detail, which dates the print and conveys the point, is the addition of a scarecrow with the profile of Bailly holding the flag of Martial Law between his teeth (La Fayette's profile is used for the crane's head). Bailly and La Fayette were the civil and military authorities in charge of law and order in Paris. They decreed martial law and ordered the shooting of demonstrators at the Champ de Mars on 17 July 1791. The demonstration was calling for the proclamation of a Republic after the King's arrest at Varennes. The journalist A.J. Gorsas commenting on the constitutional crisis arising out of Varennes in his *Courrier*

de Paris of 28 June 1791 wrote that it was "better to have a stick of a King than a Republican crane". The *bon mot* often repeated and quoted in the Assembly, probably inspired the cartoonist. Here though the sarcasm is directed at the two upholders of law and order. Its message is that the Paris people should trust neither La Fayette nor Bailly. Whilst the national guards jump like frogs to attention under the leadership of a greedy La Fayette, Bailly the scarecrow mayor is unable to protect the national poultry yard from birds of prey (including bats...) about to descend upon it. In the foreground two patriot cockrels are shown fighting each other (a reference to the split between *Jacobins* and *Feuillants*?). The cartoon is by a trained hand. The sketchy vivaciousness of the pond and yard scene recalls St Aubin, but the general treatment owes much to a design from Sebastien Leclerc (no 108 of his *Oeuvres choisies*, Paris 1784). Particular skill is shown in the sketching of the tiny frogs which are made to behave like human beings whilst retaining their animal characteristics: note the four shown standing in military poses on the log – an allusion to the replacement of the King's own guard by *Garde Nationale*. Within a life-like setting, humour and satire are conveyed by the detail. The likeness of profiles ensures immediate identification. In using English, the cartoonist pays hommage to English satirical prints, very popular during the whole period, but inspiration and treatment are characteristically French.

63

Untitled / *journée du 17 juillet. 1791, ... songez qu'il faudra Du courage pour tue' ces gens la*
Stipple; Pl. 16, 8 x 12, 6; Des. 15, 2 x 10, 5
Unsigned [Strack?], undated [summer 1791]

The design shows a flock of turkeys led into battle by La Fayette riding a prancing horse. The turkeys represent the National Guard gathering up courage as they are about to engage the demonstrators ("ces gens la") at the Champ de Mars on 17 July 1791. The "*Autel de la patrie*", still standing from the previous year is shown on the right hand side in the background. The regimented turkeys are a trope long associated with soldiers marching to slaughter: they feature in a cartoon on the expulsion of British troops from Granada dating from the campaign in the West Indies (1779) – note that one of the turkeys wears dragoon boots. The sharp angular treatment of the figure of La Fayette, the square design, the sinister use of dark shading suggest an attribution to Strack, (cf. Carnavalet, 1977 no 10).

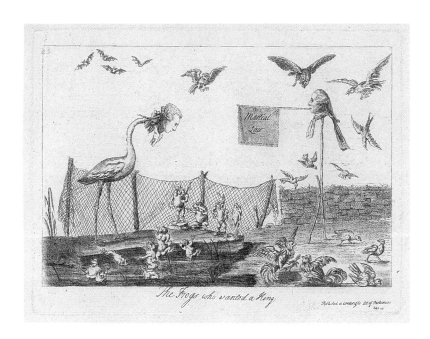

The Frogs who wanted a King

Published according to Act of Parliament

62

63

journée du 17 juillet, 1791,
Songez qu'il faudra
Du courage
pour tué ces gens là

Untitled / *l'astronome B... En observant Les astres Se Laisse tomber Dans un puits il Est tombe de Carÿbde En Scylla*
Etching and dry point, hand coloured; Pl. 15, 2 x 24, 4; Des. unruled; Wtmk [TR]
Unsigned [in corner of caption *no 8*], undated [Summer 1791]

The theme is borrowed from La Fontaine, Bk II, Fable 13, *L'Astrologue qui se laisse tomber dans un puits*. Bailly is, as the moral of the fable states 'the image of those who chase moonbeams, whilst danger threatens'. Champfleury sees in this print an allusion to Bailly's death (on 12 November 1793). By then Bailly had long ceased to be Mayor of Paris: he handed over to Pétion on 18 November 1791. The building in the background of the cartoon, as its inscription shows, is the Town Hall, and the significant detail to note is the flag hoisted up on the roof – an allusion to the red flag, the sign of the proclamation of martial law. Bailly carried it to the Champ de Mars on 17 July 1791, where under La Fayette's command the national guard suppressed a demonstration calling for the abolition of the monarchy. Bailly's role as Mayor led to his fall from popular favour. A version of this cartoon shows a path leading from the Town Hall to the well: Bailly, the Royal Astronomer as the cartoon warns, does not realise what is coming to him. A figure in the corner of the caption shows that the cartoon is part of a series. The hand which drew the lettering is also found in no 44, *Saint Pierre reniant le Pape*.

65*

Leçon donnée Par Ro ... ... / C'est semés des Perles devant les pourceaus
Etching, hand coloured; Pl. 28,6 x 20; Des. unruled; Wtmk [? FIN]
unsigned [M.A. Croisier?], undated [?late 1791]

This delicate print is a rarity. Its meaning is clear though its political intention is hard to grasp. The caption uses a quote from Matthew VII, 6 ("margaritas ante porcos", "pearls before swine") to convey the view illustrated by the image, that Robespierre's words of wisdom, his "lecon", are falling upon unworthy ears. There is no doubt that the glutton at the table represents Louis XVI, a point made plain by the animal trope of sow and piglet on the right. There is a touch of gentle satire in the figure of Robespierre: the "pearls" of his wisdom may well refer to his ornate eloquence; his well known neatness of dress, very much in Ancien Regime fashions, is high lighted by the carefuly applied bright colouring of his coat and breeches (note in particular the very unusual blue). The instrument shaped like a roman trumpet (a speaking tube) which he holds to the King's ear, undoubtedly alludes to the King's political deafness, but also clearly refers to Robespierre's notoriously weak voice. Does the cartoon intend to convey its own political lesson – that Robespierre could find a better use for his persuasive talents?

66

Untitled / *Que fais tu La Coquin? je n'ai pas de compte a vous rendre.*
Lettering behind figure on left: TRÉSORERIE NATIONALE
Etching, hand coloured; Pl. 22, 9 x 18, 4; Des. 21, 4 x 16, 5
Unsigned, undated [Oct.-Nov. 1791]

The target of this vindictive satire is Montesquiou de Fezensac, *député* of the nobility from Paris at the States General. An able economic thinker, he was a supporter of the Revolution and a promoter of the idea of a paper currency. In the great debate on the first issue of fiduciary assignats in August-September 1790 he crossed swords with Maury who cited Adam Smith to support his claim that paper money would chase specie (a point also made by Hume, the other authority quoted by some on the left e.g. Condorcet in his writings on the question). Montesquiou argued that, also according to Smith, the specie thus released would be used to purchase goods and therefore fuel economic development. Elected rapporteur of the *Comité des Finances*, Montesquiou presented on 9 Sept. 1791 the general accounts of the Treasury from May 1789. Montesquiou's ability and his commitment to reform made him a prime enemy of Ancien Régime supporters who saw in him a traitor to his class: note the word 'coquin' used in the caption, an insult usually applied by aristocrats to menial servants. Rumours were spread insinuating that his accounts were 'an imposture', that *assignats* were secretly in slush funds, and that returned assignats-bonds, were not destroyed but secreted into the pockets of Montesquiou and Treasury administrators. Asked on 1 November 1791 by the new Legislative Assembly to develop his views on finance, Montesquiou denounced these attacks 'lately read aloud at street corners'. The prints described belong to this campaign. They show Montesquiou caught in the act of rifling Treasury coffers, by a female figure in royal robes representing France. His reply given in the caption echoes the words of his 1 November speech. The several versions of this cartoon testify to the propaganda potential of the theme. One version is an aquatint printed in colour, designed in the format of book illustration. The elegant décor (curtain, clock), the inscription on the lid of the coffer, show care in finishing the design. The face of Montesquiou is clearly recognised; the abbreviated name suggests that the print is addressed to a sophisticated and knowledgeable audience. A variant was also issued in medalion. This version is an etching adapted (in reverse) from the first. The detail has been simplified and changed in a significant way. France is shown wearing a

L'astronome B.. En observant Les astres se Laisse tomber Dans un puitt
Il Est tombé de Caribde En Scilla

64

66

TRÉSORERIE
NATIONALE

Que fais tu La Coquin?   Je n'ai pas de Compte a vous rendre.

wearing a tricolour sash; crown and scepter have been omitted, gestures and postures are conventional. To make the point obvious, the designer has shown assignats stuffed in Montesquiou's pocket. The original composition has been turned into a general allegory on financial corruption linked to paper money. It is aimed at a broader public and intended to spread alarm amongst a patriot audience.

67

Untitled / LE SANS-TORT LE CHAGRIN MONTE EN CROUPE ET GALOPPE AVEC LUI
Aquatint and dry point in sepia. Plate cut; Medal 7, 4
Lettering - [on center shield:]
l'insurrection est le plus saint des devoirs/ dormez tranquile je repons de tout 5 et 6 8bre 1789 / Point de vive le vive le roy vive la Nation - [on placard:] *jugement de Mr de FAVRAS etc etc etc* - [below three sticks] *Journee du 28 F^v 1791*
Unsigned; undated, [late september-october 1791, described as on sale in JCV 26.10.91]

Another incarnation of Lafayette as man-horse (centaur = sans tort) without reproach. In format, design, use of animal persona and ultra-royalist inspiration the cartoon in the vein of no 71, and perhaps by the same artist. La Fayette is leaving the scene of his 'crimes' which are recalled by inscriptions posted up against a dark background: a shield with quotes from his most famous pronouncements and two placards recalling two counter-revolutionary episodes of his career as commanding officer of the Paris national guard: the Favras conspiracy and the meeting of armed courtiers at the Tuileries on 28 Feb. 1791 ('journée des poignards'). A cluster of sticks with severed heads, form a gruesome monument to mob rule which despite his proclaimed support for public order, La Fayette was

unable to stop: The heads belong to the three July 'martyrs' Launay, Berthier and Foulon. Leaving his alleged legacy behind him, La Fayette is represented galopping away despite the fetter on his tail, whilst 'sorrow rides behind him'. The quote is from Boileau (Epistle V) and the iconographic rendering (a devil imitating the person he possesses) echoes a long tradition of representation dating back to 16th century Lutheran prints (e.g. Cranach). La Fayette resigned his post at the head of the Garde Nationale, on the dissolution of the Constituant Assembly, and like the 'mistake-ridden fool' of Boileau returned to the country. He proposed a decree of amnesty, putting an end to all criminal proceedings relative to events of the Revolution. The general amnesty agreed by the Assembly on 14 September 1791 provided the occasion and explains the point of the cartoon.

68

Untitled / *Eh donc; coqcoco...*
Below medalion, verse of song, [twelve lines on 2 cols:] COUPLETS A MADAME COCO. AIR: OUI NOIR;. [Refrain:] *Coco, Coco, Sauvons-nous (bis) au plutot*
Lettering: 'le beau jour' on paper held by Bailly
Aquatint; etching and dry point in grey; Pl. 10, 8 x 15, 8; Medal. 7, 4
Unsigned; undated,[Oct. 1791]

In this operatic print, the first mayor of Paris Bailly and his wife are shown on stage: he reads the libretto, she is about to burst into song (the *aria* is given under the medalion). Bailly was an astronomer who married his housekeeper, a former cook: note the tools of their respective trades. An early caricature (DV 1476) mocks this domestic arrangement, and gives the couple's satirical identity of cockrel and hen. 'Coco' and 'cocotte', their nicknames were soon to follow (DV 1846). Thus typed and labelled, the Bailly are social parvenus, full of self-

esteem and mutual admiration. (The nicknames imitate baby talk and are also petnames which lovers use.) Bailly is shown carrying a 'libretto' which bears the words of his speech of welcome to the King on July 17 1789 ('what a beautiful day'). Though apparently a personal caricature, targeting Bailly's pomposity, and the couple's social pretensions, the cartoon also jeers Bailly off the political stage: his term of office is over, and the song in the caption advises him to leave Paris as a political storm is about to burst (hence the dating). The format and the visual conceit are those of the theatrical prints by Bartolozzi and Pastorini published in London in 1781, but the emphasis here is in the final analysis more political than social. The cartoon is described in JCV (23.10.91) but with a different caption. The song featured in this one was published in JCV in its number of 9.10.91.

69

Untitled / LA CONSTITUTION entre les mains de BRISSOTIN
Aquatint in grey. Pl. 7, 9 x 9, 9 : Medal. 7, 4
Unsigned; undated, [Autumn 1791]

The cartoon is an early manifestation in the campaign of vilification led by royalists against the rising political fortune of Brissot. First aimed at preventing his election to the Legislative Assembly, it was later directed at Brissot's role in the ministry. The personal gibe (note the dismissive diminutive) is aimed at Brissot's role as a jacobin journalist and at the pamphleter who made his name on the two issues of the rights of blacks and the application of the Constitution. Against an imaginary but symbolical backdrop, Brissot is shown entering the stage as a winged messenger (the bearer of news). Decor and props work by association of ideas to provide a condensed illustration of Brissot's record: he is shown toying with a yo-yo (the

LE SANS TORT

LE CHAGRIN MONTE EN CROUPE ET GALOPPE AVEC LUI

Eh donc, coq Co...

COUPLETS A MADAME CÒCO.

Air: Oui noir....

Coco, prends ta lunette,
Ne vois-tu pas, dis-moi,
L'orage qui s'apprête
Et qui gronde sur toi ;
Abandonnons Paris,
Et gagnons du pays ;
Mettons notre ménage
A l'abri de l'orage,
Dans un petit village,
Ou dans quelque hameau,
      Coco, Coco,
Sauvons-nous, (bis) au plutôt.

Je vais serrer les nippes,
Toi, serre le magot ;
Nos charges municipes,
Laissons là le tripot ;
Quittons notre palais
Et tous nos grands laquais ;
Abandonnons encore
L'écharpe tricolore,
Qui est bien te décore,
Et ton petit manteau.
      Coco, Coco,
Sauvons-nous, (bis) au plutôt.

LA CONSTITUTION entre les Mains,
de BRISSOTIN.

'*emigrette*', which becomes a fad at this time) as he does with the constitution. The leopard skin on his left arm is borrowed from 18th century iconography of African power: Brissot was the founder of the *Société des Amis des Noirs,* and in his *Lettre à Barnave* (22 Nov.1790) he attacked pro-colonists' arguments against the full application of the Constitution to the blacks in the French West Indies. The San Domingo coastline is sketched in the background of the cartoon, and the ship *l'Espérance* is an allusion to the spread of revolt in that island. The arrival of a vessel of that name at Lorient on 25 July 1791 sparked off a riot when colonial officers disembarking were seen wearing a white (royalist) rosette. The cartoon addresses the politically knowledgeable audience of cafés and clubs. Its occasion was Brissot's latest intervention in politics. When after the decrees of 15 and 16 July 1791, which exonerated the King from blame in the Varennes affair, popular pressure led the Jacobins to draft a petition asking for the King's removal, on Brissot's motion, the demand was toned down by adding the words to the draft text 'by all constitutional means'.

——

70

Les coups de Rabot [in scroll] / no caption
Aquatint and etching in grey;
Des. 28, 8 x 18, 7;
Unsigned [Webert], undated [announced as on sale in JCV 11.11 91]

——

Probably a first version of a cartoon described by Boyer de Nîmes: the background (the door of the *Manegè* where the Assembly met) is not featured here. This satirical representation of Rabaut Saint-Etienne *deputé* from Nîmes and president of the Constituant Assembly in March 1790 combines a visual pun on his name (un rabot = a plane) and traditional iconographic themes (the serpent

of heresy, speech ribbons featured in popular religious prints, Ave Marias etc). Rabaut the Protestant, in the robes of a pasteur, is busy levelling off the constitution with his plane. The wood shavings thus produced carry inscriptions listing events in the South ("Massacre de Nîmes", "Massacre d'Uzès"), anti-catholic policies ("Destruction des Prêtres"), slogans etc all imputed to a secret desire to promote his religion. A speech ribbon coming out from behind Rabaut's back proclaims that he is more venomous than a snake's ("*Je suis rampant comme le serpent mais j'ai plus de venim que lui*"). On the front of the work bench are the "five P's", a motto which southern Protestants carved on their doors ("Peuple Protestant Prend ta Peine en Patience", mocked as "Pauvre Patriote Prends Patience" in JCV 1.5.91). The cartoon makes effective use of imagery made familiar by popular prints, to focus Catholic resentment on Rabaut. *Feuille de Littérature* for November 1791 judged it "in bad taste".

——

71

Untitled / *D'Animaux malfaisants C'était un tres bon plat*
Aquatint in grey; Pl cut. Medal. 7, 7
Unsigned, undated [late 1790, on sale (JCV) 16.11.91]

——

The caption is a quotation from La Fontaine's *Fables* (Bk IX, 17). The line quoted soon became a common idiom, recorded by the *Dictionnaire* of the Academie in 1694. Here it is illustrated literally: La Fayette, Bailly the Mayor of Paris and Orléans are 'as thick as thieves'. In the fable, the action takes place between cat and monkey, the one pulling chestnuts from the fire for the other. The cartoon takes the action a step further. The wonderful little cat makes an appearance purely for fun, whilst it is the three politicians metamorphosed

into animals who do the routine: La Fayette, using Bailly as an intermediary collects the bounty from Orléans's purse. Note the use of already well-established representations of La Fayette as centaur, and of Bailly as cockrel. An early illustration of a potent theme in pro-monarchist propaganda, the cartoon presents the Revolution as led by Duc d'Orléans who fuels its fires for his own ends, with La Fayette and Bailly as his accomplices.

D'Animaux Malfaisants
C'étoit un très bon plat

70

72

Untitled/BON MOT D'UNE AMBASSADRICE.
LA REPUTATION DU GRAND GENERAL
RESSEMBLE A UNE CHANDELLE QUI NE
BRILLE QUE CHEZ LE PEUPLE ET PüE EN
S'ETEIGNANT.
Etching; Pl. 9 x 14; Des. 8, 2 x 13, 3
Unsigned, undated, [published in JCV
21.11.91]

73

Untitled / *Mr de la Fayette est Comme
une Chandelle qui ne brille que chez le
Peuple et qui pu en bonne Compagnie.*
Aquatint and dry point in grey; Pl. 9,
4 x 11, 7; Des. 8, 7 x 10
Unsigned, undated, as above.

Madame de Staël, wife of the Swedish
Ambassador and daughter of Necker is
reputed to be the author of this *bon
mot.* Her salon was frequented by leading politicians, including La Fayette.
Gossip and wit were never spared. In
the autumn of 1781 La Fayette, always a
target, drifted apart from Narbonne
(Madame de Staël's lover) after an early
rapprochement. It is known that during
their first meeting in October 1791 the
Queen and Narbonne, the minister exchanged *bon mots* and gossip about 'le
grand général'. The cartoons, however,
do not succeed in translating this particular form of salon and court humour
into visual wit and loose much of its
bite. There is no attempt at true caricature through the metamorphosis of the
object. Profiles copied from engraved
medallion portraits (cf for the aquatint,
bust portraits by Marie Anne Croisier)
are simply inserted in shapes of candle-
sticks with candles, an example of 'composition enchaînée', noted by de Caylus,
in Tome IV of his *Recueil d'Antiquités*
(1752-1767) and perhaps inspired by his
illustrations. The aquatint is the least
successful : the elegant design does little for the quip, the woollen cap which
features as the extinguisher is too re-
mote to express the comparison, the
nickname '*Coco*' added in the inscrip

tion has no point of reference in the
caption (it is usually applied to Bailly).
The etching is a better rendering : at
least, the snuffed candle is *seen* to be
stinking.

BON MOT, D'UNE AMBASSADRICE.
LA REPUTATION DU GRAND GENERAL RESSEMBLE A UNE
CHANDELLE QUI NE BRILLE QUE CHEZ LE PEUPLE
ET PÜE EN S'ÉTEIGNANT.

M.ʳ de la Fayette est comme une Chandelle qui ne brille que chez
le Peuple, et qui pûe en bonne Compagnie.

74

Untitled / Key to characters: *N I C ... us.*
2. Ch ... er. 3. Charles La ... th.
4 [inserted] Bar ... ve. 5. Brissotin.
6. Abée Fauchef. 7. Mulot. 8 Pas ... et
9 Sabot 10 Vieux Militaire 11 Groupe de
Déuté cherchant a Brissoter
Aquatint, etching and dry point; Pl. 26,
9 x 19,1; Des. 27,8 x 17,2; Reg mks;
wtmk [crown, top part of Eagle as in
Heywood 1319, Filliat?]
Unsigned [Webert], undated [on sale,
17.11.91 JCV]

This print is one of the better known
counter revolutionary cartoons produced by Michel Webert and sold at his
shop in Palais Royal. It is the first of a
number of large aquatints, elaborate in
execution, inspired in its conception by
the satirical approach and themes of the
engravings of *Actes des Apotres*. With
this print and those which follow during
the first months of the Legislative Assembly, right wing caricature comes of
age. Like all this production, this print
comments upon one of the numerous
issues debated in the Assembly, and is
rooted in a precise context. The central
character represented in the cartoon is
Camus who in August 1789, was appointed Keeper of the Constituent Assembly's archives, soon to become the
National Archives. As national archivist,
Camus was Keeper of the paper, plates
and punches used in the printing of *assignats*: note the inscription *archives
d'assignats* over the door on the left and
the trays marked *matrices d'assignats*,
shown next to it. The print comments
in high satirical language on the decision of the Assembly on 1 November
1791 to issue one million in small de-
nomination notes to be exchanged
against high value ones. Camus was
asked to release the punches used for
blind stamping the notes, against coun-
terfeiting. As usual withdrawn notes
were to be burned and to make his
point the cartoonist shows an employee
of the *caisse* burning some in the background, whilst the new notes

on Camus costume display both high
and low values and are prominently
stamped in the centre. Right wing propaganda seized on the occasion of the
new issue to launch a campaign of slan-
der against those involved in national finance questions and on prominent revolutionary figures. This cartoon shows
the arrival of the new assignats on the
scene: money is being exchanged, but
two allegorical figures hovering in the
background (Folly with her bauble, and
Opportunity emptying paper money
from a cornucopia) warn the spectator
not to fooled. Camus makes an entry
splendidly dressed up in paper money
costume (even his hair is in curl-
papers). As he comes centre stage
against the tapestry background, other
political characters rush to act out their
part: Lameth and Barnave receive back
handers, Brissot rifles Camus' coat pockets. Behind the centre group, two prominent members of the Constitutional clergy Fauchet and Mulot rush to get their
share, whilst a group of deputies (including Chabot) wait for their turn. The
loser who is shown petitioning the
group at the door is a veteran officer
wearing the cross of Chevalier de Saint
Louis. His pension not paid, he is told
to "get his next meal from his friends".
Echoing the extravagant figure of Camus
is the no less extravagant bespectacled
figure of Le Chapelier, also wearing costume and dressed up in the figures of
the gaming board of biribi, a game of
chance of the times and one which he
particularly enjoys, according to his inscription. The profiles are precisely
drawn, and dry point has been used to
underscore them (cf Chabot). In this visual extravaganza, the characters are intended to be easily identified.
The cartoon though reaches beyond
personal polemics to make a general
political comment on the value of paper
money, and on illicit gains made from
it. It does so by creating a grotesque
which immediately conveys the point,
even to an audience unfamiliar with the

inside story. The two central figures are
types representing speculation and gam-
bling, recognisable by all, as they are
modelled on the well established convention of "dress prints" showing the
trades and professions wearing the costume of their occupation (cf "Habit de
Cartier", by N. de Larmessin).

N.1 C....e. 2. Chu.....er. 3 Charles La..th..Bar...ve. 5 Brissotin. 6 Abée Fauchef. 7 Mulot. 8 Pac... e↓.9 Sabot. 10 Vieux Militaire. 11 Groupe de Députés Cherchant a Brissoter.

Untitled / *J'use tout mon Savon et ne puis vous blanchir*
Aquatint in grey, dry point; Pl. 19,
9 x 14, 9; Des. 15, 8 x 12, 7;
Wtmk: [FIN ... Ric I]
Unsigned [Webert?], undated [Autumn 1791?, on sale in Palais-Royal, 5.12.91]

After Chabroud's report to the Assembly on an investigation into the October riots (30 Sept.-1 Oct. 1790), the right wing press and pamphleteers went into 'paroxysms of rage' (W.J. Murray) against him. Chabroud's report was in fact confused and it was Mirabeau who succeeded in totally clearing d'Aiguillon, d'Orléans and Menou of any complicity in the riots. Chabroud, an avocat from Vienne and Grenoble bore the brunt of the satire, making appearances in pamphlets as 'degraisseur national' (the national cleaner) or blanchisseur (the whitewasher, cf *Faits et gestes de l'honorable Charles Chabroud ... blanchisseur du héros d'Ouersant*, Tourneux 1482) - soubriquets obviously derived from the common idiom, and given added *piquant*, by the fact that a new process for soap invented by Legendre, Orléans's surgeon was in the news at the time. The verbal gibe lends itself perfectly to a literal visual translation. Chabroud is represented holding a sponge inscribed "*raport du 5 et 6 oct*" in one hand and a bottle labelled "*savon de Grenoble*" in the other. He is attending to d'Orléans who has slipped and fallen into the mud. Dragged in the mud are the names of alleged accomplices, d'Aiguillon (called *poissarde*, i.e. fishwife, but *poix* is also pitch tar), Mirabeau and Baron de Menou. The cluster of pikes, scythe and pitchfork, and the severed heads carried off by the mud slide recall the night of October 5. On that night a mob from Paris districts (identified here as *Faubourg St Antoine* and *St Marceau*) broke into the Queen's apartments at Versailles. Several of her Guards were killed, and the heads of two of them (Deshuttes and de Varicourt) carried triumphantly at the end of sticks. On 1 April 1791, the *Journal de la Cour et de la Ville*, carried a mock report that Paris washerwomen had elected Chabroud as their Carnival King, and his reputation was further damaged later that year, by his involvement in the debates on a general amnesty.

Les Parques Nationalles Parisiennes / Pet ... Merdeux
Va ... puisque tu ne veux pas nous donner pour boire, nous allons filer ta corde parolles de ces Dames ce 17 9bre 1791
Aquatint and etching in sepia; Plate cut;
Des. 8, 5 x 10, 5
Unsigned, undated, [late November-December 1791]

A variant of the caption recorded by Bruel (DV 4066) shows this cartoon to have been intended as an insulting 'greeting card', addressing itself to Petion de Villeneuve, the new Mayor of Paris after his reception speech of 17 Nov 1791. As is often the case, reported speech, hearsay etc provide the original starting-point of the cartoonist. The not-so-veiled threats in the caption and in the action echo words allegedly spoken by street-sellers from les Halles resentful of not having been given money for a celebratory drink on the occasion. The place, a Paris street corner, with its ominous lamp-post is the common setting for acts of popular vengeance. The *topos* sends a message of warning to Petion that his popular support may soon turn against him. Petion is shown encased in a soil-tub, an image of degradation which recalls the scatological puns in the title (note the three dots and the conundrum on Maire II). The composition mixes, in its detail, realistic and vulgar touches with classical allusions. The 'Ladies' from les Halles are also the Parcae, the three Fates, and a sword of Damocles hangs over Petion's head. This mix of imagery comes from a long tradition of French political satire, dating back from the 16th century and reflects the culture of Gallican professional elites who continued to enjoy one of its favourite source-texts, *Satyre Menippée*.

Untitled / *indigestion mortel d'un
jacobin* , Dry point and roulette,
Pl. 10, 7 x 12, 6; Des. 9, 5 x 10, 5
Unsigned, undated [October 1791 –
February 1792]

Design and execution are crude: lack of
proportions, stiff outlines, poor lettering,
scratch marks all suggest a relatively un-
skilled and unsophisticated draughtsman.
The figure and the motif are awkwardly
put together. Yet the piece works as a
sort of political graffiti; unequivocal in
its sentiment and simple in its visual
message. It is clearly intended for a
popular audience. Pikes were becoming
a sign of popular revolutionary fervour
late in 1791 : Brissot published a design
in his *Patriote francais* of 26 oct 1791,
and called for the arming of the people
('*Piques* began the Revolution, *piques*
will bring it to completion'). Sparks out
of mouth are a traditional motif associated with medicine (cf 'dress prints' published by the rue Saint-Jacques e.g. the
series by N. de Larmessin). The cartoon
is occasioned by the increasingly heated
debates between pro- and anti-war factions amongst the Paris Jacobins. Fusing
together in a single image the two visual
motifs of pikes and sparks, the cartoonist
vents his anger at the Jacobins, and voices
his disgust for the Revolution.

Jndigestion mortel d'un jacobin.

78

Untitled / GARRE *aux* FAUX PAS / Key to cartoon on two cols: [left] *No1 Le Nouveau Maire densant sur la Corde II Bailli soufflant au Maire, Prends Garde au faux pas III Mr La Fayette faisant denser les marionettes IV Mr Camus Jouant du Haut Bois V Mr Brissot Jouant de la Trompette marine* [right] *VI Mmes Dondon, Picot, Stal, Condorcet donnant du Corps VII Mme Sillery, pincant la Harpe VIII Mr Dorleans jouant de la Contrebase IX Mr Villette jouant du Basson XI* [sic] *Mr Narbonne jouant la Mesure* Aquatint and etching in grey and black; Pl. 27, 7 x 19, 9; Des. 25, 6 x 17, 4; Reg. marks
Unsigned, [M. Webert], undated [December 1791; described as on sale in JCV 17.12.91]

The print is a satirical comment on the fragile political equilibrium which followed the King's acceptance of the Constitution late in 1791. It dates from the early period of Narbonne's War Ministry. Narbonne was appointed on Dec 6th 1791 and sought to broaden the constitutional majority in the Legislative Assembly by encouraging a *rapprochement* between constitutionalist factions. Brissot was active against *emigré* Princes, on the *Comité diplomatique*, and war was looming; but the issue of a Republic was apparently shelved; yet in clubs and *sections*, agitation continued and the attitude of the Municipality under the new mayor Pétion (elected on November 16th and known to have republican leanings) was perceived an important factor of the political equation. The cartoon uses the visual theme of street and musical shows to depict the political scene. The main focus in the foreground is on Pétion's aerial act. He is rope dancing, holding a balancing pole tilted on the side of a *projet républican*. La Fayette (his unlucky rival in the election) is featured as puppeteer: dressed in a coat from the dress uniform of *officier général*, but with sans culotte

trousers he operates to his own accompaniment, jigging puppets to the likeness of the King and the Queen (note though the fool's bauble). The previous mayor Bailly also makes an appearance as a political Harlequin holding a candle and puffing advice in the direction of Pétion. As expected, the street show takes place at a street corner with the facade of the Hotel de Ville as backdrop. The group depicted as musicians in the middle ground on the right, is composed of the politicians of the moment backed by their "women". The named individuals in the group are targeted as those whose interests the street trio serve and to whose political tune they perform. The right wing press jeered the personal liaisons and political influence of the high society ladies in whose salons, boudoirs or at whose dinners policy was alleged to be decided. In the back row, performing on their "corps" [cor = horn, but corps = body] are: Madame Dodun, Madame de Calon (Fauchet's mistress), Madame Condorcet and most famous of all Necker's daughter, Madame de Staël who was Narbonne's mistress. Narbonne himself conducts but centre place is reserved to the leading players, d'Orléans and his mistress, Madame Sillery, Comtesse de Genlis, known also for her talents as a harpist. From political buffoonery, the scene shifts to political intrigue. Like the little child featured in the foreground a naïve viewer may at first be entranced by the antics of the street players but as his eye would wander from the dark corner on the left along the sweep of brightly lit cobblestones towards the right, his attention would be drawn to the royal coat of arms (but with a tilted crown, and leaning republican fasces) on the front of the stand. A sophisticated viewer would then delight in the recognition of well known public figures playing in unison. This in depth composition on three planes, close medium and long range, animated by the contrasts between the blacks, the greys and the

whites thus turns the street into a stage with its forestage, wings and backdrops where a street show becomes a political performance. Using a common but fertile visual motif (performers and their acts) as its organising satirical thread, the cartoon produces a reading of politics which embodies characteristically right wing perceptions: politics are represented as play-acting; parties or groupings as *coteries*; corruption, manipulation or conspiracy (the Orleanist plot, a favourite is hinted at here) as the real explanation of situations or events. Ideas and actions are ridiculed by personal attacks founded on gossip and focused upon the foibles, peccadilloes or proclivities of public figures. Thus for instance Villette the aristocrat who welcomed the Revolution and was mercilessly attacked in right wing satirical papers such as the JCV and *Chronique scandaleuse* for his alleged homosexual tendencies, is featured here "playing with his bassoon", amongst the row of women at the back. This elaborate caricature was first announced in JCV on 4.12.91, and was on sale by 17.12.91. The artist's style identified him immediately as a master of the art: on 6.4.92, JCV announced two new cartoons (one of them *La Graine de Niais*) as also produced by "l'auteur du Faux-pas".

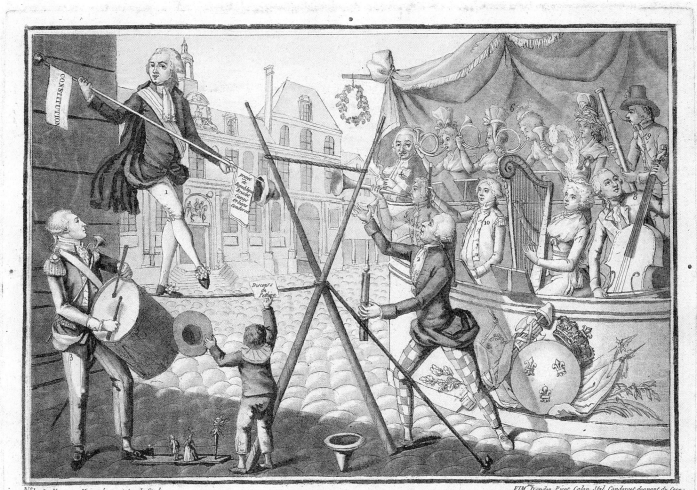

N.º1 Le Nouveau Maire dansant sur la Corde
II Bailli, soufflant au Maire, Prends garde au faux pas
III M.r la Fayette faisant danser les marionnettes
IV M. Camus Jouant du Haut Bois
V M. Brissot Jouant de la Trompette marine.

VI M. D'ondon, Picot, Calon, Stal, Condorcet donnant du Corps.
VII M.me Sillery, pinçant la harpe
VIII M. Dor'leans jouant de la Contrebase
IX M. Villette jouant du Basson
XI M. Narbonne battant la Mesure.

GARRE aux FAUX PAS.

LES COUCHES DE MR TARGET / Key to characters: *1. M. Target 2. M. L'Abbé Fauchet 3. M. Populus (P.) 4. M. d Aiguillon (S.F.) 5. Melle Theroigue (M.)*
Aquatint in grey with dry-point;
Pl. 18, 8 x 11, 4; Medal. (oval) 11, 6
Unsigned [Webert], undated [on sale (JCV) 30.11.91]

A cartoon inspired by the satirical style of the periodical *Les Actes des Apôtres* and by its attacks on the new Constitution. *Les Actes des Apôtres* derided the long process of drafting the Constitution, reporting its progress, as a court Gazette would report on a royal pregnancy. Target, a leading lawyer and member of the drafting Committee became the butt of endless jeerings from contributors to *Les Actes* who christened his expected brain-child 'la fille à Target' or 'la Targetine'. A very elaborate satirical engraving published as a frontispiece to Tome III (version troisième) of *Les Actes* makes great play of the conceit of the christening ceremony also used, much simplified, in this cartoon. The satirical motif is retained here but the detail is less flourished and the design greatly improved by the format of the group portrait. The cartoon stands on its own without the literary explanations which always accompany satirical engravings published in *Les Actes* and are written in elaborate, often laboured prose. The characters are selected from amongst the same personalities who feature regularly as whipping-boys in *Les Actes*. Shown around the baptismal fonts are: Fauchet, elected constitutional bishop on 1 April 1791 (hence his mitre); d'Aiguillon as midwife (the *Actes* latched upon his alleged taste for cross-dressing); and the two god-parents the deputy Populus and the patriot activist Théroigue de Mericourt, who became the targets in *Les Actes* of a sustained scurrilous campaign of character assassination, aimed at denigrating the morals of all those holding democratic views.

Untitled / *Sujet de la Sainte Colere de l Eveque du Calvados Contre les Pretres Refractaire...* [below caption] *Tire du Journal de la Cour et de la Ville A Paris chez les Marchands de Nouveautes / l'Auteur rue de Chabanois no 36*
Aquatint and etching in grey and black;
Pl. 15, 4 x 19; Des. 14, 1 x 15, 2
Unsigned [Webert]; undated [November 1791, described as on sale in JCV, 25.11.1791]

The scene is set in the apartments of Anne Henriette Hoquet, Madame de Calon, rue de Chabanois no 36 (cf the mock address in the caption). Mme de Calon was the mistress of Abbé Fauchet, a constitutionalist priest recently elected Bishop of Calvados and consecrated in Paris on 11 April 1791 (note his jacobin hat and his crozier under the settee). He is shown discovering his lover in a compromising position with a singer. The cartoon is in the format of book illustrations and parodies a common genre scene 'Lovers surprised', of the type designed by illustrators of Restif de la Bretonne, eg Moreau le Jeune and Leroy, but not in their elaborate style. Bergère, draperies and open door belong to the standard decor of cruder erotic vignettes and the lovers' poses could easily be retouched, as was often done to make them obscene. Fauchet's amours were the source of jokes and gossip in the *Journal de la Cour et de la Ville,* and the cartoon points to this source of inspiration in its caption. This personal satire also has a political edge: Fauchet's first pastoral letter against non juror priests created a furore in his new diocese. His pose, hair and oddly shaped right hand give him a devil-like look — his nickname in JCV is *Bouche d'Enfer*. A modified version of article 11 of the Declaration of Human Rights inscribed on the paper in Mme de Calon's right hand proposes the lesson that freedom of thought is nothing else but a licence to do as one pleases.

Les Couches de Mr. Target.

Quel soulagement

1. M. Target. 2. M. l'Abbé Fauchet. 3. M. Populus (P.) 4. M. d'Aiguillon (J.P.) 5. Mlle Théroigne (M.)

Sujet de la Sainte Colère de l'Evêque du Calvados Contre les
Prêtres Réfractaires?....

Tiré du Journal de la Cour et de la Ville.
A Paris Chez les Marchands de Nouveautés.
Editeur rue de Chabanois N.º 56.

FAIT HISTORIQUE ARRIVé A AVIGNON /
[caption on 4 lines] *On voit l Escalier
du Chateau d'Avignon, sur lequel sont les
soldats Brigands de jourdan qui casent
la tête ou égorgent les prisonniers...* [ends]
*Cette scene horrible est éclairée par les
flambeaux que des brigands tiennent
dont ils brulent la figure des prisonniers*
Aquatint and etching in grey; Pl. 28,
8 x 19, 5; Des. 27 x 16, 8; Wtmk [Dovecot,
Heawood no 1234, Auvergne]
Unsigned, undated [December 91-January
92]

Untitled / *Les Braves brigands d Avignon*
[Key under caption] *No 1. R .... bt 2. B
... che 3. C ... us.*
Aquatint and etching in grey; Pl. 23,
7 x 17, 9; Des. 22, 1 x 14, 9; Reg. mks
Unsigned [Webert], undated [announced
as newly published in JCV 18.12.91]

In towns of the South, Avignon, Carpen-
tres, Nîmes and Uzès, municipal politics
combined with religious and social an-
tagonisms, led to a number of violent
conflicts. There were clashes between
peasants and nobles, armed revolutionary bands ('brigands'), national guards
and royal troops. The events at Avignon were amongst the few – before the
Vendée – to be perceived as of national
importance. Early in 1790, the situation
in this papal possession was a subject of
fierce debate in the Assembly between
supporters of a reunion with France and
defenders of papal rights. Camus, Rabaut Saint-Etienne and Bouche, député
of Aix, were amongst the former, the
fiery Abbé Maury, a député from Comtat-
Venaissin and a relentless defender of
the Ancient Regime, led the others. The
pro-reunion party was supported in
Tournal's *Courrier d Avignon* (the journalist shown in the two satirical cartoons), Maury by Royou's *Ami du Roi*.
The press and debates in the Assembly
kept the issue alive in the public's mind

throughout 1790-91, but it was the nature of the events which followed in
November 1791 which gave Avignon its
notorious name and its high media profile. By October 1791, a troop of some
500 'brigands' held Avignon, under their
leader Jourdan, nicknamed "Coupe-
tête". When the representatives sent by
the Legislative to take over, entered the
town they discovered a number of
corpses thrown into a cavern known as
La Glacière. These were revenge kill-
ings by Jourdan and leaders of the pro-
revolutionary group, Mande and Duprat
(also shown in the cartoon). A tribunal
was set up but after long and furious
debates, the Assembly on 19 March
1792 extended its general amnesty to
cover all 'crimes' committed until late in
1791, including those of Avignon (but
with the legal fiction that it would only
be applied after Avignon's incorporation
in the national territory).
The nature of the deed, the bloodlet-
ting, the mutilations (by both sides), the
very notion of brigands, struck a deep
chord in popular minds. The story fitted
the type of spectacular *fait-divers*, nar-
rated in chapbooks and broadsides
which attracted popular imagination. Its
potential for propaganda was obvious:
through a representation of the massa-
cres, anti-revolutionary propagandists
could arouse popular fears; by association those who supported the patriots in
Avignon, could be presented as covering up for the worst forms of violence.
The three prints described are all part of
a campaign against amnesty (carried in
the *Journal de la Cour et de la Ville*, but
also in the more moderate *Mercure de
France* and other newspapers).
No 81 uses the narrative format to
present a composite *tableau*, in a sequence which leads from the top of the
staircase on the right, through scenes of
arrest and murder, to the "glacière" on
the left. This reconstruction imitates
some of the compositions and effects
used in the pro-revolutionary commemorative prints in the series of *Tableaux*

historiques, then in progress (though in
the less fine and less meticulous medium of the aquatint). The setting is accurate (note the November sky, the leaf-
less plane trees), the juxtaposition
selective. The dramatic effect is reinforced by contrasts of light and darkness, and by the mutilated body in the
foreground. A long explanation in the
caption, tells the story in eloquent
tones.
The satirical cartoon, *Les Braves Brigands
d Avignon* is more original and more
polemical. The cartoonist does not describe events, he evokes revolutionary
violence in the person of the main participants. Jourdan, Mande and Duprat
are typed: hair standing on end, wild
eyed, one moves to the kill, cutlass in
hand, the others devour limbs. Butchery
has become personified through the
typification of attitudes. Viewed globally
as dark shapes 'cut out' against a plain
white background, they form a group-
icon of revolutionary violence – visual
echoes of which (the anthroprophagi)
will reach the English cartoonist Gillray.
Closer viewing reveals more pointed
political intentions. Using variations of
tone, the cartoonist has highlighted the
main group which includes a kneeling
figure, not as might first be reckoned a
victim about to be slaughtered, but the
journalist Tournal taking notes (notice
his "trade" dress made up of the sheets
of his paper). A more shadowy group
stands behind the 'brigands'; it is made
up of the politicians who in various
postures of congratulatory welcome,
show their support to the 'brigands'.
The speech bubbles stage their cynical
exchange – with puns on Bouche's
name (bouche = mouth), and it is this
cynism which the cartoonist wishes to
expose, as he denounces revolutionary
violence. In contrast the heap of severed limbs and heads under Jourdan's
feet, has a serene classical quality in imitation of the antique style, as practised
by the painter Sauvage. The cartoonist
has altogether dispensed with historical

On voit l'Escalier du Château d'Avignon, sur lequel sont les soldats Brigands de Jourdan qui Casent la tête ou egorgent les prisoniers, on voit des brigands qui entraînent par les pieds ou par les Cheveux, à moitié mort ou tout a fait mort vis a vis est une glaciere autour de laquelle sont les brigands qui jettent les morts dans la glaciere, on voit une femme morte et son fils a genou qui demande grace mais un des boureau le preud par son habit et le jette vivant dans la glaciere, un juge paroit au fond de la cour, a qui l'on amene un prisonier, le juge dit Justice a la loi et il est austlot asome, Cette scene horible est eclairee par les flambeaux que des brigands tiennent dont ils brulent la figure des prisoniers

veracity – his intention is not to move, but create revulsion and to stir up hatred against the Revolution. The picture verifies its own truth: all those associated with the Avignon affair (even the protestants of Nîmes, la Vaunage and la Gardonenque, who were not involved but are named in an inscription) share in the collective guilt. The cartoon is a successful piece of propaganda, creating an image of broad and immediate appeal, which sums up revolutionary violence, whilst at the same time offering an exposé of the journalist and députés who condone it.

The impact of the cartoon can be measured by a third aquatint, a reversed and adapted copy of the first (not shown). Its format suggests that it was intended as an illustration. The group design has been retained, but squashed; the importance of the subtle use of half tones which conveyed the political lesson, and reinforced the facial expressions, has been missed. The addition of a cloudy sky spoils the eerie effect which the blank space has in the model. The postures are awkward: Bouche and Rabaut look as if they were collaring Jourdan. Whether or not this was the intention, this production testifies to the success of the original design in its typing of the brigands d'Avignon.

Les braves Brigands d'Avignon

N.º 1. Ra...bt. 2. Bo...che 3. C....us.

Untitled / caption in cartouche, centre of design: *son Patriotisme est en canelle*. Aquatint and etching in sepia; Pl. 12, 6 x 20, 5; Des. 11, 2 x 18, 4; Wtmk Unsigned, with a spurious address: *Au Coq-André, Rue de la Grande Tuanderie*, undated [late December 1791, early January 1792]

The figure satirised in this cartoon was the target of both left wing and right wing newspapers. D'André was a former office-holder from the Parlement de Provence and a *député* to the Constituant Assembly, elected by the nobility of Aix. A constitutionalist, he retired from politics and acquired an important grocery business in Paris. *Le Père Duchesne* attacked him as the anti-patriot editor of a newssheet *Le Chant du Coq* (Tourneux 10691): in an article of late September 1791, on the end of the Constituant Assembly and on the 'coming reign of patriotism', the radical newspaper welcomed the disappearance of "the damned crowing cockrel" and recommended that it should be used 'to wrap up the pepper-corns' of its grocer-editor. The quip probably inspired a medalion aquatint which shows d'André at his counter with a cockrel resting its paw on a copy of the newssheet (Bibl. Nat. Qbl 101259). For the right wing press d'André, nobleman turned grocer and *privilégié* turned constitutionalist, was a case of double *dérogeance*. Both *L'Ami du Roi* and *Journal de la Cour et de la Ville* make fun of him, the latter issuing a mock advertisement for d'André's shop, complete with design for his trade mark, a cockrel pecking at grapes (23.10.91). The same JCV announces in its number of 29.12.1791, Villeneuve's caricature of d'André as sugar loaf (see n 84*). Like the medalion, Villeneuve's visual conceit uses for caption "son patriotisme est en canelle", an idiom which means to be reduced to nothing (like cinnamon bark, crushed into powder by grocers...). The visual

aptness of the phrase and the comic potential offered by d'André's new occupation partly explains why satirists of all sides selected d'André as a target. The medalion was first reported in *Feuille de Littérature* for November 1791 and said to have met with "prodigious sales". Commercial success was clearly a further incentive. This cartoon uses the format of trade prints in a manner which deliberately evokes shop sign designs. It shares many jokes (including the caption) with the aquatint, and like it contrasts in its allusions, d'André's past and present occupations. It is particularly imaginative in its use of background showing d'André surrounded by labelled drawers containing spices and *douceurs* (as were given to *Ancien Régime* judges) flavoured with political allusions (*bonbon au dauphin, elixir royal* etc). But contrary to the medalion, the scales in this cartoon are clearly tilted against *le Peuple* and on the side of *La Cour*. Furthermore the newspaper placed on the counter and which d'André uses to wrap goods is *Journal de la Cour et de la Ville*. The cartoonist is no doubt familiar with the *Journal* jokes on d'André, and also with their context, i.e. the satirical pieces which it published during the period on the shortage of such luxuries as tea, coffee and sugar (note that the scales are represented as empty, except for the inscribed paper ties). In proposing for JCV the same use as *Le Père Duchesne* did for *Chant du Coq*, the cartoonist is clearly taking sides, both against d'André and right-wing critics. The cartoon suggests that in the growing popular agitation on shortages, *Journal de la Cour et de la Ville* is acting in collusion with hoarders and speculators. This charge was also made by radicals, when sugar riots occurred in Paris in February 1792.

Au Coq-André, Rue de la grande Tuanderie.

EPICIER DROGUISTE DU CHATEAU [inside border around medalion] RUE DE LA VERRERIE AU CHANT DU COQ NUMERO VINGT CINQ MILLIONS. / [caption, four line verse] D'ANDRÉ CET ÉPICIER DE FABRIQUE NOUVELLE / POUR SON COMMERCE A TANT D'HABILETÉ, / QU'IL VIENT DE METTRE AVEC LA LIBERTÉ, / LE PATRIOTISME EN CANELLE

Aquatint printed in black, red and blue; Pl. 11, 4 x 16, 3;
Oval medal. 8, 8 x 10, 8; Reg. mks
Signed: *De la Collection des Caricatures sur la Revolution Française, de 1789.. a Paris chez Villeneuve Graveur, Rue Zacharie St Severin Maison du Passage, No 21*, undated [late 1791 announced as on sale in JCV 29.12.91]

Untitled, [inside medalion border] L'HOMME DE LA COUR 1791 / L'HOMME DU PEUPLE 1789. / [caption, three line verse] TANTOT FROID, TANTOT CHAUD, TANTOT BLANC, TANTOT NOIR, / A DROITE MAINTENANT, MAIS AUTREFOIS Á GAUCHE, / JE VOUS DISOIS BON JOUR, ET JE VOUS DIS BON SOIR.

Aquatint in red and grey; Pl. 15 x 11;
Oval medal. 8, 8 x 10, 8; Reg. mks
Signed [as above], undated [? late 1791]

Two *portraits-charge* from Villeneuve's series *Collection generale des Caricatures sur la Revolution ...*, first advertised on 9.5.1791 in *Révolutions de France et de Brabant*. Their numbers [98 and 100, Tome I] are inscribed in the top corners of the plates. The first is a caricature of André, the *député* turned grocer (see no 83). André's profile is copied from a portrait *au physionotrace*. It is inscribed inside an oval itself set inside the cone of a sugar loaf. André's "trade sign", the crowing cock, is perched on top of the medalion. An inscription inside it advertises groceries sold by André, an ironic list which includes products in short supply and which insinuates that he is hoarding them (*Huile, Savon, Eau-de-vie, Sucre et Casse accaparè*).

Wrapped around the most part of the sugar loaf is a sheet of wrapping paper shown in blue: A clever image, creating the impression of a monumental sugar confection, and suggesting that André wraps the tricolour around himself the better to protect his speculation on grocery shortages.

The target of the second caricature is Barnave, the député from Grenoble (note the mountains in the background). The two-faced portrait is a familiar device used to attack duplicity, double dealings, or a political pair (La Fayette and Bailly). Here it is a representation of Barnave's apparently sudden change of political attitude after Varennes: under each foot is a paper upon which the two Barnaves tread: the bright side of Barnave, the man of the people has his foot on *Faveur de la Cour*, the dark side on *Patrie, Liberté, Vertu* – a clever idea which renders well Barnave's sudden volte-face. Villeneuve's ability shines in his treatment of the figure of Barnave. He shows the body in a pose which is naturally asymetrical; the legs and above all the gestures of arms; the arms complement each other in such a way as to evoke a recognisable pose, that of swordsman or dancer at rest. Each gesture is nevertheless sufficient to denote singly, on the one hand determination, on the other servility. An efficient use of symbolical props on each side associates the gestures with the two sides of Barnave's political personality: hat and cockade on the revolutionary side, a bag of money on his Court side. Inscriptions on the papers shown on his left recall Barnave's early record: he was a prime mover of the oath of the Tennis Court on 20 June and a supporter of the Declaration of Human Rights. Those on the ribbons around the bag in his right hand refer to his speech of 24 September 1791 which led to the deferment of a previous decree on the colonies, and to his report after Varennes where he defended the inviolability of the King.

ETRENNE AUX FIDELLES 1792 / [long caption in the form of a prayer to a saint, begins:] SAINT VÉTO MARTIR ... / *patron des emigrands et des refractaires* / ORAISON [ends:] *secrette, avec certains Décrets de l'Assemblée secondez nous De certains Décrets de l'Assemblée delivrez nous.*

Aquatint and etching in black; Pl.14, 4 x 24,3; Des. 13 x 22,3;
Wtmk [AUVE 177?]
Signed "*Gravé à* COBLENTZ *et publiée en* FRANCE *par ordre des* PRINCES"
[? Villeneuve], undated [January 1792]

The print is a sophisticated parody of representations of saints sold as devotional keepsakes to the devout who visited shrines. Such images were usually produced either as woodcuts or coloured etchings by the Rue Saint-Jacques trade. With appropriate irony, the author has produced a fake high art imitation of what was largely a cheap popular production, which mocks the devotion surrounding the person of the King, and the faith put by *émigrés* in his executive veto. In November and December 1791, Louis blocked a number of decrees directed at *émigré* princes. A new-year giftbook, the *Almanach de Coblentz* was published in Paris by Lallemand in January 1792. It contained a garland of verse and prose offerings dedicated to the praise of the Royal family. This print is a sarcastic riposte. The parody of devotional images extends to the litany-like caption which mocks in format and style formal prayers such as invocations and secrets. The bust portrait imitates in aquatint fashionable mezzotints, providing a black halo from which Louis makes an apparition in full regalia. The treatment of the face and the use of black for effect suggest an attribution to Villeneuve.

SAINT VÉTO MARTIR....

PATRON DES ÉMIGRANDS ET DES RÉFRACTAIRES

ORAISON

GRAND SAINT, voyez à vos pieds le *CLERGÉ*, la *NOBLESSE*, et la *MAGISTRATURE* du Royaume de France implorér vôtre sainte protection, ils esperent par votre heureuse intercession, être bientôt délivrez des horreurs qu'ils endurent depuis le 14 JUILLET 1789. *(Jour à jamais exécré.)* horreurs qu'ils ont soufferts en silence.... persuader qu'ils sont ô GRAND SAINT, qu'un jour peu éloigné sans doute; vous daignerez paraître en- -vironnér de toute la Gloire celeste, pour leurs rendre des PRIVILEGES et des BIENS, dont ils ont toujours fait le plus *NOBLE USAGE*.... en même tems que vous ferez rentrer les *FACTIEUX* qui les ont humiliez dans la Fange, pour y croupir jusqu'à la fin des Ciecles. *(Ainsi soit il....)*

SECRETTE

Avec certains Décrets de l'Assemblée SECONDEZ NOUS
De certains Décrets de l'Assemblée DÉLIVREZ NOUS.

Gravé à Coblentz *et Publiez en* France *par Ordre des* PRINCES.

87

Epouventail de la NATION
Aquatint and etching in grey; Pl. 19,
7 x 15, 9; Medal. 18, 6
Unsigned [chez Lebel et Webert]; undated [announced in JCV 9.1.92]

———

La Fayette as a scarecrow, with military gear, planted on the left bank of the Rhine, scaring away a flight of winged heads, representing foreign rulers. Lettering on his scabbards: (left) *Commune de Paris, (right) Congres americain,* an allusion to his earlier career. On his backpack, *La conf[l]titution[,] la bourse ou la vie*. The device of the scarecrow is also used to satirize the Austrian commander-in-chief Bender in a pro-revolutionary cartoon of the same period. Is the inclusion of a negro's head amongst the others an allusion to the situation developing in the French West Indies?

88

Untitled / circular caption in band around medalion: *Ci devant duc d aiguillon. Passe salope*
Aquatint and dry point in grey; Pl. 8,
9 x 13, 9; medal. 7, 5
Undated [chez Webert], unsigned [on sale (JCV) 23.1.92]

———

A *portrait-charge* in the format of a topsy-turvy cameo. Reversed, it reveals the profile of Duc d'Aiguillon, his beard and insignia turning into busby and cocarde. An imaginative attack using the visual conceit of a silent riddle, alluding to d'Aiguillon's alleged participation, under disguise, in the 5-6 October assault on Versailles. The clue appears in the caption when the image is totally reversed (as were escutcheons in the case of treason). To add insult to infamy, words of abuse allegedly spoken by a Versailles guard or by Mirabeau are quoted. D'Aiguillon was one of the first nobles to join the Third-Estate on 25 June 1789, and a prominent speaker against feudal rights on 4 August. Calumnied for his actions by many nobles who could not forgive him his apparent treachery, d'Aiguillon published a letter of complaint in the *Moniteur* on 21 Jan.1790 and took an action for libel in May of the same year. There were more important figures than d'Aiguillon in the politics of early 1792, but the unfortunate duke was too good a target as the 'hermaphrodite of the Revolution' to be ignored by the cartoonists.

Epouventail de la NATION.

Ci devant duc d'aiguillon.

Passe salope

89

Grand Retour du Ministre Linotte / [Caption on 8 lines] *La bonne Stal tenant son Ministre par les lizieres lui dit d'un ton Colere...*[ends] *et apprend d'eux ce qu'on doit faire quand on est gentil homme patriote /* [Keys to cartoon on two cols] *1 le Ministre 2 la bonne Sta 3 papin Netiers 4 bella Marqueze 5 Darcono Gibralla 6 Jossano Charla 7 la Mothe des 8 une Emigree 9 Club des Jacobins 10 Club des Effeuille 11 une des Vaches du ministre 12 la Societe des Creancier 13 le Jockey constitutionnel Villette 14 fesse Mathieu Montmar* Aquatint in grey, etching and dry point; Pl. 27, 3 x 19, 9; Des. 26, 6 x 15, 5; Reg. marks; Wtmk [Crown with two swans] Unsigned ["chez Lebel"]; undated [described as on sale in JCV 14.1.92]

An elaborate and sophisticated cartoon, relying on much detail to satirise ministerial and parliamentary politics during Narbonne's ministry. The cartoon combines personal polemics with a satirical assessment of the political realities behind the news. Though topical, it also reflects an ideology, and provides an insight into the right-wing mentality which shapes it. Its form of humour, both gossipy and literate is characteristic of the one practised by the right-wing press, eg *Journal Général de la Cour et de la Ville*. Its main targets, Madame de Staël and Narbonne were selected for a sustained campaign of personal attacks by a new right-wing publication *La Correspondance politique des véritables amis du roi et de la patrie*. The campaign provides the cartoon with its starting point: Narbonne is shown held in harness by his mistress Madame de Staël, like a horse being led back to his stables, a variation on the often used trope of carriage and horses. The fiction is that of a reportage on Narbonne's arrival in Paris, but treated in the manner of an elegant vignette, like an illustration for an episode in a play. The caption adds to the theatricality of the representation, by providing the words of a speech put in the mouth of the main character Madame de Staël. The language of the caption parodies that of plays, in mock italianised style (as in JCV 19.12.91). The same form of verbal humour is featured in the funny names given to the characters listed in the caption, which includes derogatory nicknames (Villette, who rides like a constitutional jockey, Montmorency-Laval, Fesse-Mathieu the miser) and some transparent puzzles (Papin Netiers must be Necker, and Bella Marqueze Beau-Marchais). The requirement to be funny visually as well as verbally is satisfied by a number of visual jokes, some of them part of the stock-in-trade of left-wing as well as right-wing satirists: the tree featured by the side entrance of the Feuillants' building (on the left) is shown shedding its leaves (a visual echo of the clue *Effeuillé*). Narbonne's discomfiture gives him a long nose. He wears a huntsman's cap decorated with a linnet's head, his nickname (from his coat of arms); some of his entourage have heads in the shape of maybugs. These jokes are graphic transliterations of idiomatic catchphrases ("faire un long nez", "avoir une tête de linotte", "étourdi comme un harreton"), the last two meaning "scatter-brained". This verbal and visual humour is not of itself political, though it is clearly intended to demean the opponent. On the other hand, the representation of a political situation as a staged performance and of political figures as actors (note the gestures imitating stage business), the assimilation of power politics to sexual politics, reflect an ideology characteristically right-wing: it is the inheritor of the tradition of Ancien régime political debate where opinion could only be expressed through the subterfuge of imaginary situations and personifications, and treats the political process as a manipulative power game reducing ideas to personalities. This brilliant cartoon turns the reportage of a fictionalised event (Narbonne's overtures to the Feuillants did not occur immediately on his return from his visit to the frontier garrisons on 7th Jan 1792) into a condensed allegory of the politics of the time, seen from this ideological perspective. The format is that of a genre scene but within the general design of architectural views: the two buildings which frame the scene are the political high places where power resides: the space of the image is itself political. The composition divides this space into two sides along the vertical lines of the high tree and the corner of the Jacobins' building, and the distinction is reinforced by different depths of perspective, and by contrasts of tone. The left side shows the comical side of the news, ridiculing Narbonne's latest moves; on the right, on the contrary stand a group of serious men (creditors) holding documents in their hands. This alludes to issue debated at length by the Assembly in the months of January and February — how and under which conditions creditors of the State could be refunded (hence Beaumarchais's presence) – and to rumours that Narbonne used ministry funds to redeem some of his own debts. In the middle of the picture highlighted in white the arch manipulator Madame de Staël is shown, advising Narbonne "I have told you a thousand times that you will achieve nothing without the protection of the Jacobins... Do like everyone else who wants to remain in power. Consult the brave legislators... and act only on their orders...". The cartoon addresses a sophisticated audience, eager for insider stories, connaisseurs with a taste for literary parody and sophisticated graphic styles. Despite his gossip columnist approach, the cartoonist shows knowledge of the intricate political situation, and makes a serious political comment.

Grand Retour du Ministre Linotte

La bonne Sta tenant son Ministre par les Lizieres lui dit d'un ton Colère

Allegorie 16. Juin 1792. Allemande /
Duel à outrance te'l qu'il a eu lieu sur le
pont de Kee'l
below Key to cartoon: *1. Botte de*
Bender portant ce coup de jarnac. 2.
Luckner le recevant. 3. La Mule du pape,
témoin de Bender. 4. La Botte de Ma-
thieu, premier Baron Chretien témoin de
Luckner. 5. Le Marechal de Rochenbeau
qui vient pour fermer l Ecurie quand les
Chevaux sont volés. 6. Bequille du Mare-
chal. 7. le Général la Fayette qui voyant
ou le coup porte, se dispose a pleurer.
Aquatint, dry-point and etching in grey;
Pl. 18 x 12, 2; obl. Medal. 13, 1 [trace of
lines framing the medalion]
Unsigned, undated [June 1792?; short
announcement in JCV as on sale 'chez
Lebel', 25.1.92]

This particular print shows traces of reworking, no doubt in order to update it:
a title (not given in the announcement)
has been added and the verb in the
caption put in the past tense. The cartoon was originally designed in January
when it was learnt that Leopold had
named Bender, then governor of Luxemburg, as his commander in chief and
ordered him to defend the Electorate of
Trèves if the French attacked. On 16
June, after the French defeats, La Fayette who had started secret negociations
with the Austrians wrote a letter to the
Assembly attributing the worsening military situation to the indiscipline of the
troops. The cartoon jeers at the discomfiture of the French general and of the
ageing maréchal de Rochambeau
(shown with his crutch, on the left). The
duel is between Luckner, commander of
the armies of the Rhine and Bender,
and takes place on the famous bridge at
Khel which linked Strasburg with the
right bank of the Rhine. The composition depicts the duel as a kind of equestrian ballet, a form of entertainment associated with state occasions, and
increasingly popular as a circus act. In
the centre group, the cartoonist has

shown instead of riders, high riding
boots (the *allemande* of the title,
though it is also a dance). This visual
motif is repeated, serving as a 'peg' for a
number of puns connected with the
meaning of the French word *botte* or of
related idiomatic phrases. *Botte* means
"Kick", including the legendary "Kick of
the Pope's mule" (but *mule* is also a
type of slipper ... note the elegant leg
on the left of the main group); *botte* is
also a *'coup'*, a thrust, a fencing movement: in a celebrated sixteenth-century
duel, Jarnac (quoted in the key) severed
the tendons of his adversary (note
where Bender's boot strikes at Luckner's).
In this riding boot fantasy, the cartoonist
plants a number of riddle-like visual
puns, inciting the viewer to exercise his
wit and to·play a game of visual and
verbal associations.

Untitled / ACTIVITÉ CONSTITUTIONELLE.
de la Municipalité de Paris.
Lettering [on sheet of paper at the feet
of Pétion] *tout est perdu adieu le Comité*
de Constitution [on letter held by Pé-
tion] *Coblentz le 10 Janvier 1792*
Aquatint and dry point in grey:
Pl. 11, 1 x 13, 9; Medal 9, 5 diam.
Unsigned [chez Lebel], undated ['newly
appeared', JCV 28.1.92].

The Mayor of Paris Pétion is shown
caught in obvious discomfort, his pants
undone, sitting on a commode and
about to make use of the sheet of paper
he holds in his hand. Another sheet lies
already discarded, at his feet. Inscriptions – *Coblentz le 10 janvier 1792* and
tout est perdu le Comité de Constitution,
explain the reason for his embarrassment. On 1 January 1792 after lengthy
debates, the Assembly pronounced an
act of indictment against the Princes and
émigré leaders gathered at Coblenz who
had refused an ultimatum to disperse.
Brissot the leader of the pro-war party
claimed that *la peur que fait Coblentz*
was the cause of the Assembly's pro-
crastinations, calling upon revolutionaries "not to soil themselves" by inconse-
quent actions"...! The theme was seized
upon by right wing cartoonists who began, around this period, to make use of
scatology for satire, as pro-revolutionary
cartoonists (such as "A.P.") had done
earlier on. When the cartoon appeared,
letters by *émigrés*, indicating that they
were about to seize some towns, had
been made public. In its brief description of the cartoon, JCV commented that
news from Coblenz had the same drastic
effect on the Assembly as the improved
rhubarb plant with which it had been
presented some weeks earlier. Another
satire on Pétion (*Encore une fois, Garre*
aux faux Pas) in the same economical
style is announced with this one in JCV.

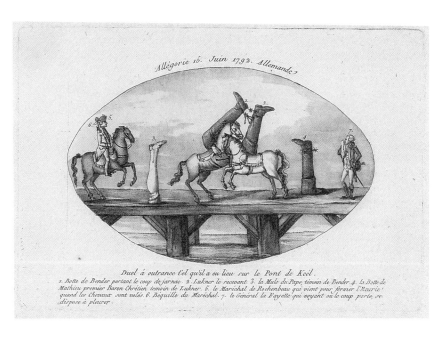

Allégorie 16. Juin 1792. Allemande?

Duel à outrance tel qu'il a eu lieu sur le Pont de Keel.

1. Botte de Bender portant le coup de jarnac. 2. Lukner le recevant. 3. la Mule du Pape, témoin de Bender. 4. La Botte de Mathieu premier Baron Chrétien témoin de Lukner. 5. le Maréchal de Rochenbeau qui vient pour fermer l'Ecurie quand les Chevaux sont volés. 6. Béquille du Maréchal. 7. le Général la Fayette qui voyant ou le coup porte, se dispose à pleurer.

ACTIVITE CONSTITUTIONELLE
de la Municipalité de Paris.

Untitled / *Grande Seance aux Jacobins en janvier 1792, ou l'on voit le grand effet interieure que fit l'anonce de la guerre par le Ministre Linote a la suite de son grand tour qu'il venoit de faire*
Aquatint and etching; Pl. 21, 8 x 16, 9; Des. 20 x 13, 7
Signed: *Vilette invenit* [a spurious signature], undated [available chez Lebel, JCV 1.2.92]

This cartoon parodies the tableau genre, or the commemorative print – in this case perhaps an etching by Masquelier. No such meeting actually occurred in January 1792, though the issue of going to war was hotly debated in the *Société des amis de la Constitution* known as *Club des Jacobins*. Narbonne (the linnet head) and his maybug aids (centre, around the stove) were not members, neither was La Fayette whose name is inscribed on the snake's tongue in the right-hand border. Mirabeau's bust was placed over the President's desk in the Club, but there is no mention in any source of the allegorical figure of time shown here. The description of this cartoon given by *Journal de la Cour et de la Ville* helps to put names on the four speakers shown (with speech ribbons) at the rostrum: they are from left to right Brissot (*guerre ouverte*), Condorcet (*horrida bella*), Herault de Sechelles ("bataille") and Robespierre (*il est urgent Mrs que nous fassions semblant de n avoir pas peur*). The border of snakes added to the tableau is a clear signal that its intention is satirical though this only fully emerges after closer attention to detail. The numerous lightly sketched figures with which the cartoonist has peopled his tableau seem to invite this kind of scrutiny. Contemporary *connaisseurs* would have been drawn into it by the discovery of the many expressions achieved by skilful flicks and nicks, in the sketching of noses, eyes and particularly mouths. Scrutiny of the detail then reveals the scatological motif – a number of deputies

have soiled their pants. Undoubtedly, informed readers of *Actes des Apôtres Journal de la Cour et de la Ville* would have taken the hint from the spurious attribution to Villette. Villette, the "marquis back to front" is the character who is featured lowering his trousers and showing his posterior in another cartoon ("Abus constitutionel", no 120). In this cartoon the President of the session is represented in a similar posture. He is Mathieu de Montmorency, another target of the right wing press, known as *Fesse Mathieu* (Slap-bottom). Behind him, Teroigne and other revolutionary ladies try to help him in his moment of embarrassment (*le cas est embarassant*). The cartoonist has scattered other such representations amongst his *Jacobins*, some easy, some made less easy to spot. This scatological tableau is intended to represent, as hinted in the caption, the drastic effect (*le grand effet interieur*) that the growing likelihood of war was reputed to have had on those who had clamoured for it.

93*

Untitled / TIENT VOILA MONSIEUR DEPIBALLE
Aquatint in grey and dry point.
Pl. 13, 8 x 19, 9; Des. 11, 9 x 17, 5;
Reg. marks.
Unsigned [label], [announced in JCV 6.2.92]

The character has been 'snapped' unexpectedly in a comic posture. The look of surprise and recognition suggests that artist and subject are acquainted. A true personal caricature, in a tradition going back to Ghezzi? There is individuality in eyes, mouth and body, but the quasi-simian face and general stance belong to the stereotype of age. The figure is not so much in the likeness of a person, but in the manner of a comic stage character in military costume, playing at being a soldier but ill-suited to the role.

Note the comic effect of the huge hat, the long coat, the out of scale weapons. The detail (rosette) and decor (wainscoting, drapes with royal arms) give the game away; the stage-property and the gesture (à la Hogarth) tell the political lesson. The cartoon mocks the Garde Nationale as a 'Dad's army', ill-suited to protect the King and warns that it is there to spy on him and that it cannot be trusted.

Grande Séance aux Jacobins en janvier 1792, ou l'on voit le grand effet intérieure que fit l'anonce de la guerre par le Ministre Linote a la suite de son grand tour qu'il venoit de faire

94

DOMINE SALVUM FAC REGNUM / [Key on two cols] *A Buste de Louis XVI. Emblème de la Royauté. B Personnage connu qui veut s emparer du Throne apres l'avoir renversé. C Satellites de ce personnage. D le Fameux coupe tête E la France est écrasée sous les debris du Throne. F Mgr le Pce de Condé qui jure de mourir pour venger la Royauté. G autres princes du sang faisant le meme serment. H Neker et Ce souriant à ce desastre. I le Prince de C...i se reposant du tout sur l honneur des autres* Aquatint and etching in sepia; Pl. 26, 7 x 20, 6; Des. 24, 9 x 16, 4 Unsigned ["chez Lebel"], undated [described as on sale in JCV 7.2.92]

The cartoon borrows its format, composition and manner from historical tableaux, of the type shown in *salons* by academiciens such as La Grenée the elder. It depicts a fictional scene of heroic action, where the Princes unite to repulse an assault by an armed mob led by the 'traitor' d'Orléans and his 'henchman' Jourdan. Dramatic gestures and conventional poses convey a sense of action, though faces are expressionless (except in the case of Jourdan). Along a diagonal from left to right, the two groups face each other, in a clash between order and disorder, animated by a forward and backward movement: note in the depiction of the weapons, the parallelism of the pikes behind the group on the left, the convergence of the lines of the swords, in contrast with the multiplicity of shapes and the disarray of lines on the right. The plebeian clothes, the severed heads denote demotic rage, the drapes and the uniform, aristocratic grandeur and strength. The steps and the contrast between drapes and sky in the background create the impression of a stage construction designed to show simultaneously two locations: the street outside, the sanctuary (with Louis's bust) inside. Two figures stand out from the main groups: the intruder d'Orléans shown stepping on a dislocated stone from the steps, and the defender Condé coming down to confront him and ready to strike him with his fist. The action is arranged as if viewed from the right-hand bottom corner. The low angle selected enables the artist to use the device of the steps to place the left-hand group in a dominant position and convey the impression of a surge forward, a movement made manifest also by the posture of the recoiling figure, detached from the right-hand group and seen from the back, which occupies the bottom right-hand corner of the picture. In the foreground, France is shown as a fallen female figure covering her head with a cloth, with the cockrel and the oak leaves symbolizing the valour of its ancient monarchy. The allegory both points to the situation and calls for action. Altogether the cartoon is an eloquent visual rendering of the cry "God save the Kingdom" used for its title. The phrase is adapted from the one which was uttered aloud in unison by a congregation at the end of religious ceremonies where the King was present (Domine salvum fac *regem*). The change in the traditional wording, the representation of the Monarchy not in the person of the King but by an 'emblem' are not without political significance. Early in December the Princes rejected a lukewarm appeal by Louis to return to France. Louis's intervention though prompted by the tense political situation, lost him support amongst ultra monarchists. The cartoonist's choice of wording and image place him in this 'ultra' camp, as do the two satirical touches he has added to an otherwise stirring image: on the left he shows the Prince of Conti asleep in an armchair, whilst the throne is in danger; and in the wings, we see a group of constitutional monarchists (Narbonne with his customary linnet head, Necker & others) waiting for a favourable outcome which would install d'Orléans as regent, and lead to the establishment of a bicameral system of government.

DOMINE SALVUM FAC REGNUM.

A. *Buste de Louis XVI. Emblême de la Royauté.*

B. *Personnage connu qui veut s'emparer du Throne après l'avoir renversé.)*

C. *Satellites de ce personnage.*

D. *le Fameux coupe tête.*

E. *la France est écrasée sous les debris du Throne.*

F. *Mgr. le Pce de Condé qui jure de Mourir pour venger la Royauté.*

G. *autres princes du Sang faisant le même Serment.*

H. *Neker et Ce. Souriant à ce desastre.*

I. *Le Prince de C...i se reposant du tout sur l'honneur des autres.*

94

*La Bascule Patriotique / Il est Claire que
le Nouveau Regime emporte la Balance*
[below caption, Key to cartoon]
Nu⁰1 La Peste 2 La Guerre 3 La Famine
Aquatint in sepia; line engraving; Pl. 15,
7 x 11, 6; Des. 14, 9 x 9, 8; Reg. marks
[Wtmk: Auv[ergne] 178[?]]
Signed *au Palais Royale chez Webert N⁰
203*, undated [announced in JCV 7.2.92]

A rather ambiguous cartoon. The device
of the see-saw features in a number of
cartoons, some in popular style, and is
used to illustrate the new political (or
social) equilibrium. Here its application
is far from explicit: The three harpies
are conventional representations of the
three evils from which the people
prayed to be delivered, war, famine and
pestilence (in the Roman ritual, 'a peste,
a bello, a fame'). The allegory of the
National Assembly with a book (the
Constitution) in place of head is not
very successful. Crozier, scepter swords
and sabers are the trappings of the Ancien régime suppressed by the new
one, but they are shown sticking out of
a bundle which the figure carries over
her shoulder, as thieves would do. Are
they her loot? The stick showing from
under her left arm is decorated with
paper money. In her left hand she holds
a bottle of poison, labelled Aqua de fana
[for 'fanatisme'?], and in her right hand
what looks like a sponge. The detail is
not clear, however, and the objects on
the right could be cobbles or stones. The
design is muddled, but the caption must
be ironical. Boyer-Brun describes this
cartoon (TI p 159), but with variants and
speaks of 'a bottle of poison'. The print
in the De Vinck collection is unsigned,
but the address on the Chester Beatty
print, makes it clear that the intention is
satirical, as Webert had monarchist sympathies. On the other hand, the cartoon
may just allude to the late revision of
Constitution, this 'new regime', which
Prud'homme in his *Révolution de Paris*
considered viable provided 'a sponge
was drawn' over the past.

Untitled / *Grands Envoyés Extraordi-
naires de leurs Majestes les Jacobins pour
le Blanchissage, de Jourdans, et son armée, leurs Confraires.*
Lettering in background [on door] *un
moment Messieurs je suis votre chef je
dois passer le Premier* [over figure of
gaoler] *Ordre du Roi* [on window] *a moi
Chabroud Blanchisez moi* Lettering on
objects [held by Bouche:] *its seront
bientot Blanchi* [in Chabroud's hands]
éponge Fine [on floor] *c essance de Savon
Savons de Grenoble CB Eponge Fine*
Aquatint, etching and dry point in grey;
Pl. 19,7 x 15,6; Des 18,7 x 13,2;
Reg. mks
Unsigned [Webert], undated [announced
in JCV 16.12.91]

Ultras were outraged by the proposed
extension of the general amnesty to "Les
Brigands d'Avignon" in December 1791.
In this cartoon Jourdan and his men are
shown behind bars, and about to be released, as Chabroud and Bouche prepare to shitewash them. They are
shown carrying washing paraphernalia
(a washerwoman's beetle, a wash-bowl,
a sponge). In the fore and middle
grounds, a tub of liquid soap and a box
of cakes of soap (from Grenoble, Chabroud's town) help to provide perspective. Chains, bars, locks and keys (with
gaoler) denote that the scene is set in a
prison. The artist makes good use of
aquatint tone combined with geometric
patterns to create atmosphere. The light
shines on the faces of the gaoler and on
the two main characters through the
barred window on the right. Close ex-
amination of the inscription on its bars
shows that the words "amort["death to..."]
have been altered to "amoi" ["help me"].
Originally, as is consistent with light and
perspective, the faces at the window
were intended to represent people
shouting for Jourdan's head (he is
shown locked behind the gaol's door).
The alteration was made at the caption
stage, perhaps in anticipation of violent
popular reactions.

La Bascule Patriotique

Il est Claire que le Nouveau Regime emporte la Balance
Nu.º 1. la Peste 2. la Guerre 3. la Famine
au Palais Royale Chez Weber, N.º 203

Grands Envoyes Extraordinaire de leur Majestes les Jacobins pour le Blanchissage, de Jourdans, et son armée, leurs Confraires.

decouverte faite par le cousin Jaques /
DEUX PENDUS DANS LA LUNE
Aquatint in grey; Pl. 16, 9 x 22, 3;
Des. 14, 7 x 18, 3;
Wtmk [AUVERGNE]; Reg. mks; [in top
right hand corner:] No 2
Signed with spurious address "*Se trouve
à Paris au Département et à Metz au
Quartier Général* [in reality, Webert],
undated [announced as published in
JCV 16.2.92]

Cousin Jaques is the *nom de plume* of
the right-wing publicist Beffroy de Reig-
ny, who published various newspapers;
his *Nouvelles Lunes du Cousin Jaques*
appeared during the second half of
1791. He is shown looking through a
telescope at the moon on the face of
which the silhouettes of two men hanging can be seen. They can be identified
as La Fayette and Bailly from inscriptions around the edge of the moon from
the dates inscribed on the hanging
frames and by their dress. La Fayette is
in his uniform of commanding officer,
Bailly wears his mayoral sash (hence
the mock address). The inscriptions
quote their famous sayings – La Fayette's
"l'insurrection est le plus saint des de-
voirs", Bailly's "la publicité est la sauve-
garde du peuple". Dates refer to the
"Journée des poignards" and the
"Champ de Mars" affairs. This elegant
print is a clever allegory on the role of
public opinion (the telescope through
which Cousin Jaques contemplates the
moon) and an attack on La Fayette and
Bailly as arch manipulators who will
one day pay for their crimes. The engraved number on the print indicates
that it is a re-issue of one published in
January, probably as part of a *collection
complète des caricatures*, which was
announced in *Journal du Peuple* of
5 March 1792.

*Le pouvoir Exécutif à cheval sur la Con-
stitution; / Casse col des Jacobins en at-
tendant &c &c &c...*
Aquatint in sepia; Pl. 17, 2 x 12; Medal.
14, 4 x 9, 1
Unsigned [Lebel]; undated [announced
in JCV 11.2.92]

The visual theme is borrowed from
chap-book illustrations of *Les Quatre
Fils Aymon,* one of the best selling
prose romances published in *Bibliothèque Bleue.* Riding on their Constitutional horse are Louis, Narbonne [in his
linnet persona] and two other ministers,
probably de Moleville and de Lessart;
they did not agree with Narbonne on
the need for ministers to consult the Assembly Committees, and were denounced in the Assembly. At the beginning of February Marie-Antoinette wrote
to de Mercy that there was 'open war-
fare' in the ministry, hence the cartoon
which shows Louis and his ministers
"riding for a fall". Note the horse's head
which recalls *Départ du Général Parisien.*

la Balance de Thémis.

les pauvres petits protestans tirent, les grands philosophes soulevent: mais hélas! le tout en vain.
N.º 1. Vincens, Plauchut 2. Jeannot preyre 3. Brissot 4. Condorcet.

Cat. Rue de Francs(ques) XVI siecle.   Se trouve au Palais Royal chez Webert N.º 203.

101

102

ADORATION DES PATRIOTES, a l'aspect d'un gros.
Sous, dessinée en france d'apres nature L'an (Sans argent)
3 de la liberté.

103

Untitled/ NOUS VENONS QUI
L'EMPORTERA.
Key to characters: *1 La Constitution /
2 J Petion Maire II de Paris /
3 Factieux dits Jacobins*
Etching; Pl. 35 x 22; Wtmk
[large Badefaud?]
Unsigned; Undated [described as
published JCV 15.3.92]

A reworking in the popular manner of a
well known aquatint. The composition
is on a larger scale and the contours are
crude. A child-like naked figure has been
added falling head first behind the left
group - an awkward symmetry attempting to balance the towering Hercules on
the right. The figures bear no resem-
blance to the model: they look like an
assemblage of standard designs (monks,
knights, the beast) from models for
cheap cut-out prints. The monster-rider
group is out of proportion and uses the
standard representation of the famous
Hyene du Gevaudan The caption is new
and reproduces a hand-written inser-
tion, noted by Bruel as added in pen to
the aquatint in the De Vinck collection.
The register is more popular and the
print has a touch of bravado absent
from the model. The profile of Petion is
hardly a likeness. The stereotyping of
attitudes, the standard panoply, both
simplify and amplify the attack, and the
etching is more direct in its call to action.
More propaganda than satire, it is likely
to be destined to audiences unfamiliar
except in general terms with its model's
specific target.

104

Untitled / *Grand Maître de l'ordre du
Cordon gris, en habit de Cérémonie.*
Aquatint in grey, dry point and etching;
Pl. 18, 11, 1; Medal. 13, 8 x 9, 1
Unsigned, undated [stated as on sale in
JCV 27.3.92]

The sparse graphic design creates a
starkly visual image intended not to
amuse but to jeer and to threaten. The
cartoon dates from a new sustained
campaign of vilification led by ultra royalists against d'Orléans, during the early
months of 1792. Here he is shown going to the scaffold, in the familiar group
representation of executioner and victim.
Orléans is dressed in the humiliating
habit of criminals (with the cap which
was the headgear of convicts and later
became a revolutionary symbol). He
was one of the first aristocrats to discard
royal orders insignia and the cartoon
represents him girded with rope and
adorned with miniature scaffolds and
ladders, in lieu of the blue ribbon and
cross of Ordre du Saint Esprit. Thus at-
tired he belongs to the confraternity of
the doomed, on their day of reckoning
as in Houdard de la Motte's well-known
lines, Fables (V, 20): "C'était la fatale
journée / Où l'ordre de la destinée / Lui
faisait prendre l'habit gris ...". The *lavis*
manner achieves subtle variations of
grey tone adding to atmosphere and to
symbolic meaning. Sarcasm is present in
the gesture of the fierce looking hang-
man, holding Orléans's coat-tail, as in a
mock procession. An ominous touch is
added to this sinister scene by the dark
and menacing shadow appearing on the
wall.

NOUS VERRONS QUI L'EMPORTERA.

1 La Constitution.
2 J. Pétion Maire de Paris.
3 Factieux, dit Jacobins.
4 Le Boulanger accompagné d'Hercule.

103

orlé. s   bour.

Grand Maître de l'ordre du Cordon gris, en habit de Cérémonie.

104

Untitled / D'UN TAS DE FUMIER, LES JAC-
OBINS TIRENT UN MINISTRE DE LA GUERRE
/ [lettering on cartoon] *Ministre de la
guerre* / ECURIE D'ORLEANS
Aquatint in grey, etching and dry-point;
Pl. 22, 8 x 16; Des. 21, 2 x 13, 2
Signed: Grave sculpt, undated ['newly
issued', JCV 23.3.1792]

The cartoon makes use of the conventions of 'views' and monumental prints
or illustrations of town buildings, increasingly fashionable in the late 18th
century (plates for the major series *Voyage pittoresque de la France* began to
appear in 1784). Most of the space is
taken up by a side view of the
d'Orléans main stables, in a perspective
which accurately shows the long and
stern facade and highlights its monumental central porch (designed by Poyet
and built in 1778). The usual scene from
street life intended to bring animation to
the architectural view is present, but
larger in proportions than expected in
order to make the political point. Men
are busy clearing a heap of manure and
loading it on a cart under supervision.
This lowly task, reserved for labourers
contrasts with the grand classical decor
of the porch and with the elegant figures of lad and horse on the right. One
of the group holds up a notice to draw
the viewer's attention to a derisory figure pulled out of the heap: a derogatory
respresentation of the Jacobins (in their
usual personae of monks in habits) and
of Grave (whose appointment to the
ministry was engineered by the Giron-
dins) engaged in d'Orléan's dirty work.
The signature is fanciful (cf DV 4476).
The *Journal de la Cour et de la Ville*
states that the cartoon is by *l'auteur du
Faux Pas*.

Untitled / LE MINISTRE GRAVE. *Repen-
dant ses bienfaits sur ses protecteurs*.
Aquatint and etching in grey; Pl. 19,
9 x 15, 2; Medal. 15 x 10, 8
Unsigned [Webert]; undated [March
1792; described as on sale in JP 27.3.92]

Grave became minister of war on March
13 and was replaced by Servan on May
8. Madame Roland later said of him that
'he lacked ideas... and lost his head in
the midst of his department's business'.
A political non-entity, Grave seems to
have been preoccupied with two immediate issues: the distribution of gun
powder and weapons to municipalities
and the settlement of pensions to former royal officers belonging to the
Order of Saint Louis. He was opposed
to the former, and in favour of the latter. The royalist cartoonist represents
him as an ineffectual mountbank dish-
ing out crosses and wine to claimants.
Note the derisory comment on Grave's
ministerial performance provided by the
little dog lifting his leg against the
bench (perhaps a draughtsman's mark,
reappearing on several cartoons, including one issued after Fleurus by Martinet).
Though the visual theme and composition used (the street scene) are conventional, the group on the left is a sharply
drawn representation of the populace as
a rabble. The device of showing Grave's
head inside a bottle became Grave's
satirical emblem during his short public
career. It may reflect comments such as
those of Madame Roland, and echoes
the nickname of *Girondiste*, coming into
use to designate the group of deputies
from the South West who assert their influence with the creation of the first parliamentary ministry. The cartoonist, unable to precisely situate Grave politically,
just hints at the association. He was
however well informed about ministerial
business, as the two issues which occupied Grave were not yet discussed in
the Assembly when the cartoon appeared.

D'UN TAS DE FUMIER, LES JACOBINS TIRENT UN MINISTRE DE LA GUERRE.

LE MINISTRE GRAVE.

Répendant ses bienfaits sur ses protecteurs.

Duel à outrance / Suite du Duel le 2 Mars 1792. La Bonne Cause triomphe, la Pique nous assure la Victoire.
Key to characters [left to right] *2. Robespierre, Jacobin 1. l Empereur Feuillant.*
Aquatint, dry-point and etching in sepia; Pl. 25, 3 x 18, 1; Des. 22, 1 x 15, 6; Wtmk
Unsigned, undated [described in JP 24.3.92]

It is not clear which triumph or which cause the cartoon claims to celebrate. After the first ultimatum to Austria (on 25 Jan 1792) Robespierre multiplied his warnings against the dangers of going to war. They were directed both against the Feuillants and against Brissot's 'Girondin' party. He attacked the first in a speech to the Jacobins on 2 March, and clashed violently with supporters of the pro-war Girondin in his *Address* to the Jacobins of 26 March. The idea that in moving towards war, the Feuillants served Emperor Leopold's interests could have some credibility early in March, but when the cartoon appeared, Leopold's death (which occurred on 1 March) was known in Paris, and pro-war Jacobins had replaced Feuillants in government. In his 26 March *Address* Robespierre described Leopold's death as a providential act, and as a further cause for peace. The cartoon represents him in an exaggerated fighting pose; his attire and the curious bow in his hair give him a puerile appearance. The inscription on his pike ("liberty or death") and the quote from the Declaration of Human Rights on his shield, identify him as a champion of the Revolution, in keeping with Robespierre's self-appointed role (he was called "le vigilant"). The other figure is a composite picture of Leopold in *Feuillant* robes – a cardboard-like figure in the posture of defense, holding his globe as if it was a rock about to be thrown. The cartoon could have been designed originally to jeer at Robespierre's attack against the *Feuillants*, by representing it in the mock heroic manner. As events made it less relevant, caption and title may have been adapted to retain some topicality: the 'extravagant duel' may mock Robespierrre's persistence in continuing the fight after the disappearance of his antagonists – a triumph, no doubt, but not of his cause, nor of his own making. The point remains unclear and its attribution to a 'marquis a rebours' (probably de Villette) in *Journal du Peuple* does not help.

Regeneration du Capucin Chabot. / Ou alliez vous Mᵉ l Abbé.
Aquatint, etching and dry-point in sepia; Pl. 12, 6 x 16, 9 [trace of another impression 11, 7 x 16, 2]; Des. 10, 7 x 13, 6 Unsigned [Webert?], undated [described as published in JCV 5.2.92]

In late January 1792 the *Journal de la Cour et de la Ville* begins to publish mock news bulletins on Chabot's health. Chabot was unwell during the preceding weeks, though he attended meetings of the Assembly and spoke on important financial matters. This crude attack on Chabot is clearly inspired by the satirical jibes in JCV. In the cartoon Chabot is shown subjected to the standard treatment for syphilis, i.e. the use of preparations of mercury (hence the winged messenger and his caducea): baths of diluted solutions of perchloride of mercury (corrosive sublimate) were used, as well as injections and pills. The various forms of treatment for syphilis are represented in the cartoon; the *pilules de Belost* may be the equivalent of the famous Guy's Pill, though Belost was also a legendary poisoner of the late XVIIth century. The treatment was painful and one of the effects of mercurials was to cause abundant salivation (shown here in the form of a speech scroll coming out of Chabot's mouth). In the inscription Chabot complains that he is "pierced to the marrows", a direct echo of a double-entendre used by JCV in its first February number. The strange saucepan in which Chabot lies is a visual rendering of the common phrase for this type of treatment ("passer à la casserole"). This 'poisoned' cartoon does not conceal its disgust for Chabot as a person, and for his new life as defrocked monk (note Chabot's capuchin beard and the friar's habit and scourge lying on the floor).

Duel à Outrance

2. Robospierre, Jacobin.　Suite du Duel le 2 Mars 1792.　1. l'Empereur Feuillant.
La Bonne Cause triomphe, la Pique nous assure la Victoire.

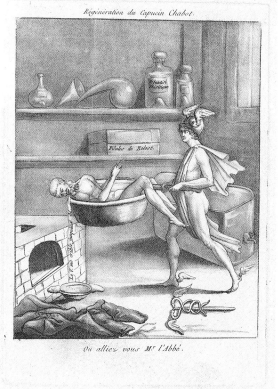

Régénération du Capucin Chabot.

Ou alliez vous Mr. l'Abbé.

le degel de la nation / *Le milieu du tab-*
leau est occupé par un morceau
d'immondices pétrifiées par l'air, sur
lequel les sans culotte ont élevé la statue
de la Nation et de la Liberté. L'instant
que nous avons saisi est celui où l'air se
radoucissant, on voit la statue fondre
insensiblement. Déja le bonnet dit de la
liberté s'enfonce dans le crane amolli de
la statue... ses bras sont tombés, elle n'est
meme plus da plomb. En vain les sans
culotte souffflent-t'ils pour maintenir
leur ridicule ouvrage, le Soleil Royal, par
son influence rend leurs efforts inutiles:
ils sont dans l'eau et dans la fange à mi
jambe. Déjà aussi les tombereaux font
leurs offices, les conducteurs y jettent in-
distinctement avec leurs pelles et les bras
de la nation qui sont à terre, feuillants,
jacobins et autres clubistes pour aller
avec le reste des ordures, attendre leurs
confreres, où ... à la V ... Sur un terrain
élevé, nombre d'honnetes gens réunis
applaudissent à la justice céleste qui en
fait une si eclatante de toutes ces turpi-
tudes populaire.
Aquatint, etching and dry point in grey;
Pl. 32, 3 x 26, 7; Des. 30 x 21, 4;
Reg. mks; Wtmk [FIN DE C. FILHAT, cf
name of countermark in Heywood no
1319]
Unsigned [Webert?}, undated
[announced JCV 19.3.92]

This allegorical tableau shows a statue
(the Nation as Liberty wearing her cap)
melting down under the Royal Sun.
Rubbish carried by the thaw is accumu-
lating at the foot of the statue, and the
patriots who built it are slipping and
falling into the muck as they attempt to
run away before it collapses. The centre
of the composition is occupied by the
curious representation of a statue without arms tilting sidewise and back-
wards, as if to avoid the warm rays of
the sun. The scene is intended to represent a 'snow woman' melting under the
spring sun: note the men busy cleaning
up and loading a dirt cart on the right –
a very seasonal activity. Yet the statue
has the shaped body and garments of
wax models popular at the time.
Marked contrasts of tone emphasize the
briskly sketched characters grouped
around the figure. The two comic figures blowing on their bellows on the
right are Fauchet and Carra. In the foreground the cartoon highlights a figure
sprawled in the muck and clinging to a
sheet of paper – the recently elected
Procureur-général de la Commune,
Pierre Manuel. Manuel's office gave him
control of the Paris police, long the ennemies of the print trade. Here though
he is selected for scornful treatment as
the supporter of sans culottes and the
recent author of an insolent pamphlet to
the King which began with the words
"Sire je n'aime pas les Rois" (shown in
the inscription). Webert, from whose
shop the print undoubtedly originates,
also settles old scores with Revolutionary journalists by also including in the
débacle Desmoulins (editor of *Révolu-*
tions de France et de Brabant) and
Prud'homme (editor of *Révolutions de*
Paris). The composition is structured
like a diorama leaving space for two
groups in the middle ground: on the left
a rabble marching to the rescue. On the
right, seen from below in an elevated
position a view of the Royal family with
honnêtes gens watching the scene from
the terrace of the Tuileries. The background is used for a topical allusion
which grounds for those in the know
this curious visual eschatology in a precise political context. The cartoonist has
shown Narboone riding off to Metz.
This is an allusion to the events of
March 10, when the King, having dismissed Narbonne, sent Grave's nomination to the Assembly. On the same day,
a letter from Narbonne asking permission to visit the frontier post of Metz
was read to the Assembly. Two speech
scrolls escaping from the horse's rear
and the rider's mouth read "mon maître
n'est pas assez grave" and "je vais rendre mon compte a Metz" – the latter an
ironical summary of the contents of Narbonne's letter, and of his journey, which
was seen by his ennemies as an excuse
to avoid submitting the accounts of his
ministry. This fusion of allegory and
topicality is not unique to right-wing
propaganda, though it is particularly significant in this print: Narbonne's dismissal was seen by royalists as a sign that
the King was at last taking the initiative
and eliminating pro-revolutionary ministers. In the Assembly the Girondin party
denounced "a system of intrigue design
to go back on the Revolution and to
modify the Constitution". This print is
evidence of a resurgence of pro-royalist
propaganda during the spring of 1792,
directing itself to amplifying by allegory
the hopes of a constitutional crisis
which combined with war would lead
to the collapse of the Revolution.

Le milieu du tableau est occupé par un monceau d'immondices pétrifiées par l'air, sur lequel les sans culotte ont élevé la statue de la Nation et de la Liberté. L'instant que nous avons saisi est celui où l'air se radoucissant, on voit la statue fondre insensiblement. Déja le bonnet dit de la liberté s'enfonce dans le crane amolli de la statue..... ses bras sont tombés, elle n'est meme plus da plomb. En vain les sans culotte soufflent-t'ils pour maintenir leur ridicule ouvrage. Le Soleil Royal, par son influence rend leurs efforts inutiles : ils sont dans l'eau et dans la fange à mi jambe. Déja aussi les tombereaux font leurs offices, les conducteurs y jettent indistinctement avec leurs pelles et les bras de la nation qui sont à terre, feuillans, jacobins et autres clubistes pour aller avec le reste des ordures, attendre leurs confreres, où.....à la V......
Sur un terrein élevé, nombre d'honnetes gens réunis applaudissent à la justice céleste qui en fait une si éclatante de toutes ces turpitude populaire.

Untitled / *Essai de la Guillotine.*
[in speech ribbons from left to right] *je men vas en canelle – je denonce – gâre mon compte – dormez tranquilles – Paris a reconquis son Roi – ma chere targetine* [foreground] *Ah Coco* [figure of Orléans under guillotine] *malgré chabroud* [judge-executioner on the right] *je n'ai pas changé de metier.*
Etching with grey wash [? trial proof];
Pl. cut; Des. 22, 9 x 14, 3
Unsigned, undated [April 1792]

This curious print, wishfully surrenders to trials of the guillotine leading consti-tutionalists and opponents of the abso-lute monarchy. Leading the group in chains is Target holding his pet child the Constitution. He is followed by Bailly holding the Keys to the city of Paris, then by La Fayette, Montesquiou, Danton (?) as a tiger figure and André as cockrel. The upright speech ribbons by which the characters are identified, show English influence, as does the linear sketchy outline. The focus is on the guillotine (with a conventional not realistically shaped blade) and on d'Orléans about to be dispatched by the judge-executioner: the executioner still has a job to do, despite Chabroud's dismissal of early conspiracy charges against d'Orléans. In the foreground Madame Bailly in her well-established turkey persona. Technically, the print appears unfinished and the use of grey wash conceals a good deal of smudges from a dirty plate.

Untitled / [4 line verse] *Grand Dieu de quel cote que je tourne mes pas // je vois la honte et le suplice; // Ah! si j'avais du Coeur, je n'hesiterais pas // A rendre au monde un grand service.* [on two cols, key to cartoon] *1. L'Espagne fait le signe de la Croix; comme pour l Exorciser 2. l Allemagne figuree par un Aigle qui fond sur lui 3. le Pape et ses Cardinaux, le poursuivant a coup de Crosse 4. le Danois ... l Abboyant... 5. la Suisse et la Savoie disent: ne recevons que d bonnetes gens. 6. la Hollande = mauvaise marchandise 7. l Angleterre: Figure par le leopard et deux autres betes feroces s opposant a son passage 8. Blanchard lui offre de le derober a la juste fureur de ses ennemis.*
Aquatint and dry point in grey; Pl. 26, 8 x 19, 7; Des. 25 x 16, 2; Wtmk
Unsigned [?Webert], Undated [April 1792, announced in JCV 9.4.92]

An attack on the character and actions of Philippe, Duc d'Orléans. As Duc de Chartres, in his young days, Orléans was known for his carriage driving skills; in July 1784 he had taken part from Saint Cloud in a first attempt at dirigible ballooning. Later to protect himself against allegations that he had participated in the October days, he left France for England on 14 October 1789, on a fictitious mission set up by La Fayette and the King. He returned without permission on 7 July 1790 to clear his name, as the Chatelet tribunal was about to indict him. Character assination of the Duke began early, but the royalist campaign against him reached a climax early in 1792. Calumny is the main weapon here: the hares which draw the chariot are traditional emblems of cowardice (an accusation already levelled at him after the Saint Cloud flight and the Ouessant fiasco). This visually prolix print shows him being rejected by the European powers and attributes to their collective opprobrium his despair.

Graphically the cartoon is a pot-pourri of motifs and subjects made fasionable by English satirical prints of the period (ballooning, carriage driving, national types), with a mixture of allegorical and emblematic devices, whilst the overall design is in the manner of topographical aquatints, and the scenery inspired by mountain views as depicted in the *Tableau ou Voyage pittoresque de la Suisse* or by Ballini in designs engraved by Auvrayon or Née for the Dauphiné volume of *Voyage pittoresque de la France* (1784).

1. *l'Espagne, fait le Signe de la Croix, Comme pour l'Enterrer.*
2. *L'Allemagne, figurée par un Aigle, qui fond sur lui.*
3. *le Pape et ses Cardinaux, le poursuivent a coup de Crosse.*
4. *le Danois ... l'Aboyant ...*
5. *le Suisse et le Suisse, chient ; se resserre qui il chancelle, gene.*

Grand Dieu de quel coté que je tourne mes pas
je vois la honte et le Supplice ;
Ah ! si j'avais du Cœur, je n'hesiterais pas
A rendre au monde un grand Service.

6. *la Hollande, mauvaise marchandise.*
7. *l'Angleterre, figurée par le leopard, et deux autres bêtes féroces empoisonnant a son passage.*
8. *Blanchard lui offre de le dérober a la juste fureur de ses ennemis.*

112

les loups ne se mangent point. / LES
JACOBINS LAVENT LEURS CONFRERES
GALERIENS, SOLDATS DE CHATEAU VIEUX
[Key to characters] *1. Soldats chateau
Vieux 2. S. Huruge 3. Fauchef
4. Villette 5. Brissot 6. Chabot*
Aquatint and etching in grey; Pl. 19,
5 x 15, 4; Des. 17, 9 x 12, 5;
Wtmk [De?z?ner]; Reg. mks
Unsigned, undated [described as on sale
in JP 17.4.92 and in JCV 18.4.92]

On 17 April 1792, a public ceremony
took place in Paris in honour of the
Swiss guards from the regiment of Lullin
de Chateauvieux who had been par-
doned by the *Legislative*. The guards
belonged to one of the three standing
regiments stationed in Nancy who had
mutinied in August 1790 against harsh
discipline and the appropriation by their
officers of regimental funds. The rebellion was put down by Bouillé, some of
the rebels were executed, others
(shown here) sent to the galleys. The
Jacobin Sillery produced a report to the
Constituant Assembly critical of Bouillé's
actions and repeated calls were made
for a pardon, eventually granted by the
Legislative in application of the general
amnesty late in 1791. The pardon and
the ceremony outraged monarchists and
moderates (amongst them the poet
A. Chénier who denounced the idea in
Journal de Paris of 9.3 and 4.4 1792).
The cartoonist does not conceal his
scorn for the guards: the scroll they
hold blatantly proclaims that they stole
regimental funds. He uses a familiar
satirical theme (whitewashing) but in a
design remarkable for its composition,
sense of detail and animation. The centre
of the picture is occupied by a realistic
representation of washer room equip-
ment: note the hugh vat, the ladles, the
laundry basket on which Fauchet, bishop
of Calvados (hence its inscription) is
made to stand. Postures and gestures in
the centre group reveal the eagerness
with which they perform the white

washing ceremony. The snapshot effect
is achieved by the positioning of the
guards, of the Jacobin group in the
background and of the figure of Villette
with magnifying glass, depicted as moving into the frame of the picture. Jacobin
hats with huge rosettes and military
caps in darker shade form a motif
which gives unity and atmosphere to
the scene. The cartoon has uncommon
features: the care shown in the variety
of expressions depicted in the faces,
and the treatment in quasi-transparency
of two frieze-like designs: one, on the
side of the vat shows the heads of
Launay, Flesselles, Berthier and Foulon,
the first "martirs de la revolution"; the
other on the back wall, shows three
Ancien Régime instruments of execution
– a hint that the Swiss guards and their
Jacobin protectors deserve no better,
and a bitter comment on Jacobin sense
of justice (Fauchet is "faux-chef", a
hypocrite to the core).

113

Untitled / LE GARDE NATIONALE
*revenant des frontieres, Cocu, battu et
content.*
Aquatint and etching in sepia; Pl. 10,
1 x 17, 3; Medal. 9, 3
Unsigned, undated, [April 1792,
announced in JCV 26.4.92]

The cartoon gloats over the early defeats
suffered by the French armies during
the spring of 1792. Against a hilly background (the Argonne region on the
Eastern frontier?), with a scene of cavalry
routing infantry, attention is focused on
the derisory image of a volunteer subjected to humiliating treatment. The
image of a dog relieving himself against
the *garde's* valid leg belongs to the traditional stock of visual *facetiae*. The
boy applying boot polish to the *garde's*
wooden leg is a visual rendering of a
common proverbial saying. The caption
is also a common idiomatic phrase. The
cartoon uses the iconographic conventions of a traditional genre (proverbs-
into-images) to make its political point.

LE GARDE NATIONALE

Revenant des frontieres, Cocu,
battu et Content.

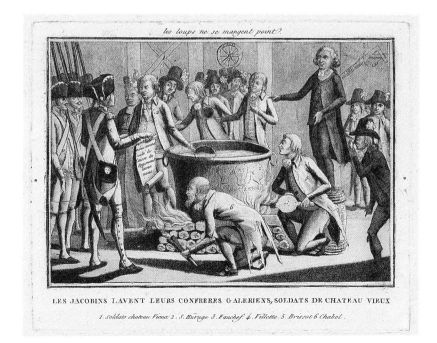

les loups ne se mangent point.

LES JACOBINS LAVENT LEURS CONFRERES GALERIENS, SOLDATS DE CHATEAU VIEUX

1. Soldats chateau Vieux 2 . S. Huruge 3 . Fauchet. 4 . Pillotte. 5 . Brissot 6 . Chabot .

114*

Héritiers de la Constitution. /
LES MALHEURS DE LA FRANCE FURENT
LEURS OUVRAGES [below] *La rage*
l erreur et la cupïdité enfantrent ces
mons ... s.
Key to cartoon [on two cols beside
caption]: *a. Chap .. er biribi. b. Targ.t. c.*
Lecou .. ux. d. Cam .. e. Bar .. ve f. Lam.
th. g. Guill .. me. h. Le Duc d or ... s i. La
france. k. Neker.
Aquatint and etching in grey; Pl. 27,
6 x 20, 3; Des. 25, 7 x 17, 3; Wtmk
[...BAL..? ...ARS...?]; Reg. mks
Unsigned [Campion], undated [on sale,
JP 6.4.92]

This satirical print is amongst the best
produced by right wing cartoonists.
Much thought was given to its conception and design. It was announced in
JCV on 12 February 1792, but only appeared in April. Its execution with use
of stopping out and with much lettering
required time and several impressions
were needed (note the registration
marks). In its composition, mix of realism and fantasy, use of tone, and in the
full use made of the entire surface of
the plate it recalls the manner and treatment of two others *Domine Salvum Fac
Regnum* and "*L'Homme aux Assignats*",
most likely produced by the same artist.
This print combines the format of the
group portrait (such as those of echevins
or guilds) and that of the illustration of
plays, contrasting and connecting the
quiet pilfering on the left with the violent robbery on the right. A common
theme, the financial rewards of the
Revolution, is illustrated in the posed
portraiture on the left and in the staged
action on the right: The scene on the
right – France attacked by d'Orléans
and Necker – represents the blatant
plundering of the monarchy, the group
on the left – the quiet sharing of the
proceeds by the Constitutionalists. Their
group portrait is ordained so as to show
the principal "beneficiaries" Target and
Camus seated at a notaire's desk, whilst

standing behind them Le Chapelier,
Lecouteux, Lameth and Barnave delicately pass around envelopes (a symbol
for bribery): note the movement of
hands. Representations of money provide a common referential point: the
National Treasury chest filled with assignats in the foreground on the left echoes
the bag of bills and coins marked "Tresor
Royal" rifled by Necker on the right.
The link between the early and the
more recent events of the Revolution is
provided by a trio of intermediaries depicted in the middle ground at the centre: Lameth notices the assault but still
collects his bribe; Barnave "l homme a
deux faces" looks as usual both ways.
The third figure in military uniform is
Guillaume, the former dragoon from the
Queen's own regiment who arrested the
royal fugitives at Varennes in the name
of the Assembly. In the background,
two sets of painting put the scene in its
historical context: the "legitimate" face
of the Revolution is shown in the two
portraits of the Paris Mayors Bailli and
Pétion; its ugly face in the two tableaux
with title and name of "artist" depicting
the two events which are the key to the
new state of affairs: the arrest at Vare-
nens, *Guillaume pinxit* (note how its
'author' points proudly at his work) and
the forced signing of the Constitution
(*signe aussi non De Fay pinxit*). Unlike
most other cartoons which simply target
some of the key political actors, this remarkable print succeeds in providing in
condensed form and in tight format, a
full visual exposé of the Revolution,
depicting simultaneously three of its
key aspects which are visually and thus
causally inter-connected. It embodies a
view of the recent history of France, inspired by a traditional right wing sense
of outrage. But like "l'homme aux assignats", the print puts a new stress on
financial gain as the main motivation of
leading revolutionaries – a good propaganda theme given the increasingly serious financial problems which faced the
Legislative. As visual propaganda the

cartoon is particularly well conceived: it
combines the emotive appeal of dramatic allegory, the sophisticated satire of
known public figures, and quotes from
Revolutionary iconography (portraits
and tableaux) in order to subvert it.

115

*Grande Colere du Dieu La Fayette lors
de l'affaire de Verdun / Paroles
qu'adressa le Gal Blondinel au Regt de
Piémont, qui refusèrent de lui rendre
hommage (Ah vous voulez suivre
l'Impulsion de votre Coeur, Tremblez
devant le vainqueur du Champ de Mars)*
Aquatint, etching and dry point in grey;
Pl. 10,4 x 8,9; Des. 9.1 x 7
Unsigned, undated [January 1792]

A fine rectangular miniature, showing
particular care in the lettering of title
and caption. A minor incident is ampli-
fied in a caricature which debunks La
Fayette's arrogance and his pretensions
to be the new commander in chief. A
gunner from the *Garde Nationale* appears to set fire to La Fayette's blond wig.
The suggestion is that La Fayette is in-
censed (enflammé) by the attitude of
regular regiments (*Piedmont*) who de-
spise the national guard and refuse to
accept the authority of its former
commander.

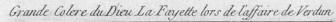

Grande Colere du Dieu La Fayette lors de l'affaire de Verdun

Paroles qu'adressa le G.ᵃˡ Blondinet au Reg.ᵗ de Piémont, qui refusérent de lui rendre hommage (Ah vous voulez suivre l'Impulsion de votre Cœur, Tremblez devant le vainqueur du Champ de Mars)

La Liberté triomphante, ou les Sans-Coeurs terrassés / Le 5 Avril l'An 4me de la liberté
Key to characters: *1 Leopold mort le 2 mars ce grand Despote dissout tous les projets / 2 Le grand Condé ne sachant ou donner de la tête / 3 Monsieur fait comme Monsieur Veto il examine / 4 Le Comte d'Artois est confondu dans la mêlée / 5 Mirabeau Tonneau perd ses forces il débonde / 6 Le Cardinal crie au secours, les siens sont empechez par leur pied de nez / 7 Toute l'armée est dans un trouble affreux appercevant les volontaires patriotes*
Aquatint and dry-point in sepia. Pl. 28, 8 x 19, 5; Des. 26, 9 x 17, 8
Unsigned, dated 5 April 1792.

A rich imagery mixing allegory and satire in a composition reminiscent of commemorative tableaux in the grand manner fills the whole space of this spectacular print. The scene is dominated by the figure of liberty rising over a battle scene; the two armies of France and the Coalition face each other on each side of the picture. The main confrontation takes place centre stage along a diagonal in the symbolic contrast of light and dark shades. Liberty a classical figure in flowing robes, the sparks of liberty crowning her head, armed with a pique with phrygian cap soars like dawn in a halo from a garland of cannon smoke. Weird and grotesque shadows, the leaders of the *émigrés*, dazzled and overwhelmed fall back in disarray. The contrast of light and darkness, the variations of scale turn this scene into a political altar piece, which focuses the attention upon the symbolic mesage.
A closer look shows the print to be more than an icon of triumphant freedom. The fallen figure dagger in hand in the left hand side foreground, apparently asleep like a soldier in Grünewald's depiction of the Resurrection, is signposted by an inscription on the flag. This is the Emperor Leopold whose sudden death on 1 March 1792, was thought to have delayed Coalition plans of military intervention against the Revolution. When decrypted the detail and the captions (repeated around each figure) turn allegory into satire, and identify the main targets: Loménie de Brienne, the Princes, Condé, Riquetti-Mirabeau. The latter two had assembled a legion and an army which they were to lead. Note the characteristic uniform of Mirabeau's legionnaires, black decorated with skulls and bones. In the centre of the human heap, the reclining figure of Provence gazes through a telescope at Liberty, unable as his brother Louis, Monsieur Veto, to make up his mind. Emigré nobles and an abbé also make up the clownerie in the foreground as they tumble over one another crushing Artois, the King's younger brother.
The cartoon is designed for immediate impact to inspire zeal, but also to generate political comment, as its audience explores and delights in the reassuring sarcasm of its detail. (Captions guide the process of explanation.) The composition succeeds in representing in a single image the main themes of patriot ideology: A quasi religious vision of revolutionary ideals, a derisory treatment of its opponents, a dismissive view of the armies of the Coalition. The context of publication brings out the propaganda value: The issue of the disbanding of émigré troops gathering on the lands of the Elector of Trèves, was the focal point of the rise in the international tension which led to war. On 17 January 1792 the Assembly learnt that Leopold had offered the protection of his army to the Elector, should the French move against him, but news of his death reached Paris on 2 April, boosting the confidence of the revolutionary party. The militarist spirit and political eschatology expressed in the print could be mistaken for triumphalist make-belief, were it not for the satire and for the popular spirit (verbal humour and street carnival) which inspires its comic representations: the émigrés' masks, their long noses (as they are "led by the nose"), Condé's Carnival hat, Mirabeau-Tonneau as a barrel debunged ('de'bonder' ='de'bander', with a further obscene meaning as you note the pose of the female figure in the group).
Above all, the print attempts to arouse the people, with the powerful image of the auxiliary army of volunteers, going into battle, featured on the right hand side. Calling the nation to arms, the cartoonist has highlighted this realistic representation of the people in arms, contrasting it with that of the Austrians, shown as puppets playing with yo-yos.

La liberté triomphante, ou les sans Cœurs terrassés.

le 5. Avril l'An 4.me de la liberté.

117

Banque de Vauvineux / LA GRAINE DE
NIAIS
Key to characters: *1. Vauvineux*
*2. Condor... 3. Briss... 4. Compére etc
etc...* Lettering [on banner.] *a vis Louis
d'Or a Dix sols en echange d'Assignats.
Banque Francoise avis aux actennair et
porteurs de lettre de la Banque* [on
chest] *Caisse La Farge Colombals et
Courbin etc etc*
Aquatint in grey; Pl. 15, 2 x 10, 9;
Des. 14, 1 x 8, 9; Wtmk [grapes]; paper
[quarter sheet, approx. 27 x 21, 1]
Unsigned ["chez le Campion", by
l'Auteur du Faux-pas], undated
[announced as on sale in JP 7.4.92;
attribution in JCV 6.4.92]

This cartoon belongs to a series of six
aquatints satirizing the financial news of
the day, published by the artist known
as *L'Auteur du Faux pas*. His inventive-
ness in dealing with topical subjects
shows in the variety of conceits upon
which he draws to illustrate his point.
He quotes freely from many traditions,
but in a very personal style. Side views
give a sense of immediacy to his compositions, the use of shading in the ink
and pen manner creates volume and
depth. Above all he displays a mastery
of the oblong medalion format: his characters though elaborate do not cramp
the design. Setting and detail (e.g. costumes) mix the realistic with the conventional in order to add a touch of social satire to political polemics (see
Adoration des Patriotes). This cartoon
illustrates the proverbial phrase *graine
de niais* by means of a representation of
the platform performance given by a
group of travelling street sellers—a device
inspired by the Tabarin prints of the
previous centuries. Here the targets are
Vauvineux, a financial trickster and those
who fell for his bare-faced roguery.
Vauvineux is shown in splendid costume
selling "merchandise" (i.e. assignats) to
a group of stooges in the crowd (Compère
and wife). His accomplices are a Pierrot

[the 'naïve' Condorcet] with a fool's bib
and Brissot [the orator and publicist]
'trumpeting the news abroad', with lantern phrygian bonnet and rat-tail à la
Jacobin. They were the two theoreti-
cians of the emerging Girondin party,
and they feature in the cartoon, out of
pure malice. Neither supported Vauvineux's scheme when it was presented to
the Assembly in March, nor were they
taken in by the claim that it could restore
parity between specie and assignats. Denounced by many as fraudulent, the
scheme collapsed on 13 April, only a
few days after this cartoon appeared.

118

Untitled / *la pelle et les sabots, sont du
même bois.*
Key to characters: *1 Notre Dame de bon
secours 2 les Créanciers, l'an sans
argent de la Liberté*
Lettering on cartoon: [on balloon] *Proto*
[on poster] *Guillaume – tel qu'il le mer-
ite pour Défécit de trois milions* [in sky]
miserere mei l'Assem Natio [on newssheet, centre of picture] *3 milions en
papier a prendre sur le Trésor public dé-
cret du 30 mai 1792.*
Aquatint in grey; Pl. 15, 1 x 10, 9; Oval
medal. 14 x 18, 8
Unsigned ["l'Auteur du Faux-pas" JCV
6.4.92], undated [advertised as on sale at
Le Campion in JP 7.4.92]

A satire on the decision by the Assembly
on 30 March 1792 to redeem the Paris
Maison de Secours by allocating to it
funds from the Treasury. The *Maisons
de Secours* were for small depositors
and borrowers (a mix of pawnshop and
exchange bureau). They issued small
value *billets de confiance*, used for day-
to-day purchases in lieu of coinage
which was in short supply. Retailers
used them to pay suppliers who could
then exchange them back for assignats.
On March 1792 it was discovered that

Guillaume (the director) and the person-
nel of the Paris *Maison* had speculated
on the devaluation of assignats and that
assets were not sufficient to cover the
billets in circulation. The Paris municipality which had taken over the man-
agement of the *Maison de Secours* asked
the Assembly for help. The incident satirised in the cartoon was only the beginning of a long drawn out crisis which
involved provincial *Caisses* as well. All
such establishments were forbidden to
issue more billets on 30 April, and a total of 23 millions were allocated to meet
their deficit. In October 1792 the Convention was forced to step in again with
more drastic measures. The publication
of this cartoon in a series of six in
April, so close to the actual events,
shows how well informed the cartoonist
was, and how he could sense what
could move public opinion. In this cartoon he pillories Guillaume by representing him tied to a pole, whilst The
Assembly appears to him in the shape
of a Virgin and child, perhaps a quote
from an altarpiece in one of Paris
churches, but also from civic paintings
showing *échevins* and their patrons.
"L Auteur du faux pas" is a humourist:
he quotes from one of his own funny
captions (l'an / sans argent de la Liberté),
gives a nickname to his victim
(Guillaume Tell – a fashionable allusion
to Gretry's comic opera, just put on the
stage –), and amuses himself by inserting
a double visual joke in the background
of his composition: A salvage operation,
or "renflouage", is also performed on
ships (refloated) or balloons (reinflated).
In this last case, the joke receives added
piquant by recalling recent ballooning
attempts by Blanchard.

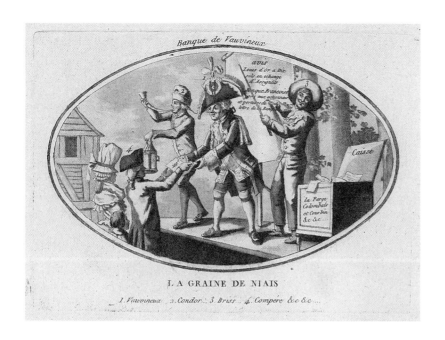

La Graine de Niais

Banque de Vauvineux

LA GRAINE DE NIAIS

1. Vauvineux.. 2. Condor.. 3. Briss.. 4. Compère &c &c..

la pelle et les sabots, sont du même bois.

1. Notre Dame de bon secours 2. les Créanciers, Un (sans argent) de la Liberté.

119*

LE NOUVEAU CALVAIRE / [Key to figures]
NI Louis seize mis en croix par les révoltés. 2. et 3 Monsieur et Monsr Comte d Artois freres du Roi lies par les Decrets des factieux 4. Robespierre a Cheval sur la constitution suivi de la gente Jacoquine presente au bout d'une pique l'Eponge Imbibée de fiel [above line with]] sign] *de ses motions régicides. 5 La Reine accablée de douleurs montre son epoux et ses freres et sollicite une prompte Vangeance. 6. la Duchesse de Polignac au pied de la croix 7 Mgnr le prince de Condé Indique s'apprête a venger son Roi.*
Aquatint, etching and dry point in black; Des. 14, 7 x 20, 3; Reg. mks
Signed "*se vend a Paris chez Webert Palais Royal galerie de bois no 203*", undated [announced as on sale JCV 26.4.92]

The idea that the Revolution is turning into a kind of Passion for the monarchy dates from the early period of the Revolution. On 12 April 1790 De Lameth denounced in the Assembly a "vile pamphlet on Louis's passion" published during Easter week. This pamphlet entitled *Passion et Mort de Louis XVI, Roi des Juifs et des Chrétiens* is a bizarre and impertinent piece ending on the execution of Clergy, Parliament and Monarchy (the scene mixing hanging and crucifixion is shown on its engraved frontispiece). In royalist propaganda the theme of the King's passion emerges after Varennes. Devout monarchists were profoundly shocked by the fact that the King was not allowed to go to Saint-Cloud on Easter Sunday 1791 to receive communion from a non-juring priest. It did not escape their notice nor that of leading revolutionaries that the incident undoubtedly influenced the King in his decision to leave the Kingdom, and that the attempted escape occurred during the feast of Corpus Christi. Robespierre who was sensitive to religious issues was amongst those who commented

upon this in speeches to the Jacobins: hence his inclusion in the print as the horseman who offers to the crucified King the sponge dipped in vinegar at the end of a reed. The crucifixion scene (contrary to the 1790 frontispiece) has all the features of traditional iconography – note the darkening sky, the grieving women, the hammer and the nails, but mixed with quotes from the panoply of revolutionary symbols – note the crosses shaped like fasces, the cap of liberty on Louis's cross, the Tables of Law. Instead of the usual Constitution and Declaration of the rights of man, these are inscribed with the words *Tables de proscription*, followed by the names of proscribed *émigré* leaders and princes. The composition is notable for the prominence assigned to Marie Antoinette as the central figure of grief (in traditional pose), and to Condé in martial pose drawing his sword. In this emotive allegory of the political calvary of the monarchy, the representation of the King's brothers as the two thieves and of Princesse de Polignac as Mary Magdalen could appear incongruous, but the print seeks not so much to elicit devotional respect and compassion as to call for revenge. As *Journal du Peuple* hopefully commented in its 26 April number, "a violent storm is about to burst" on the political scene.

120

Untitled / no caption
Lettering on scales design: [left] ABUS CONSTITUTIONEL [below] ELLE NE S'ELEVERA PAS. [right] ABUS MINISTERIELS [below] ELLE NE DESCENDRA PAS.
Key to characters [on 3 cols from left to right]: *No 1 condorcet armé d'un lévier veut en vain soulever les abus constitutionelle. 2. Villette pretant son dos pour servir d'apuy au Levier. 3 Bazire aussi armé d'un levier fait de vains effort pour soulever les Abus Constitutionels.*
4. Causon Citoyen actif et jacobin tire un cordeau qui ne peut faire descendre

les abus ministeriels. 5 Brissot ambarassé dans les cordes de Sanson. 6 Claviere imitant Sanson fait comme lui des efforts inutiles. 7 ... l'Abbé fauchef enchemise tourne un rouet dont les Cordes ne peuvent faire descendre le Coté des abus ministeriels. 8. Isnard ... portent les oeuvres de M. J Chénier pour ajouter aux poids deja attachés au coté 9. le Cointre Ministeriel de la Balance . ce volume est ce qu'ils ont trouvé de plus pesant. 10 ... Chabot sur une échelle.
Aquatint and etching in sepia; Pl. 26, 7 x 20,1; Des. 25,2 x 16,3
Signed [*se vend à Paris chez Webert Palais Royal. N 203.*], undated [announced in JCV 26.4.92]

This print uses the visual device of the scales of justice to provide a political allegory mixed with personal satire. Similarities of composition and treatment – in particular in the contrast of the scales and the diminutive characters suggest the same author as for no 102. The theme is more narrow and less immediately accessible. The print comments on the conflicts which occurred within the government and between the King and the Assembly during the period which led to Dumouriez's ministry. At issue was the question of whether the ministers were responsible to the King or to the Assembly, and more generally the working relationship between the executive and legislative branches of government. Narbonne who favoured ministerial accountability clashed with his colleagues De Molleville and De Lessart and was dismissed by the King on 9 March. Brissot and his supporters counter-attacked by accusing De Lessart of treason. The right wing press (e.g. *Correspondance politique*) saw in these conflicts first a manoeuvre by Narbonne to revise the Constitution on the English model (with a prime minister), then an attempt by Brissot and the Jacobins to suspend the King. The print argues that, despite the best efforts of a number of

elle ne descendra pas.

N.1 Condorcet armé d'un levier veut en vain soulever les abus constitutionelle.

2. Villette prêtant son dos pour servir d'apuy au Levier.

3. Baxire aussi armé d'un levier fait de vains effort pour soulever les abus Constitutionels.

4. Cauzon Citoyen actif et jacobin tire un corteau qui ne peut faire descendre des abus ministeriels.

5. Brissot embarassé dans les cordes de Sanson.

6. Claviere Imitant Sanson fait comme lui des efforts inutiles.

7. . . . . L'Abbé fauchet en chemise tourne un rouet dont les Cordes ne peuvent faire descendre le Cote des abus ministeriels.

8. Jenard, portent les oeuvres de M. J. Chénier pour ajouter aux poids déja attachés au coté.

9. le Cointre, Ministeriel de la Balance, ce volume est-ce qu'ils ont trouve de plus pesant.

10 . . . . Chabot sur une echelle.

se vend a Paris chez Webert Palais Royal N. 203.

120

Jacobins, the wrongs done to the Constitution far outweigh those done by the Ministry. To this general political lesson, the cartoonist has added touches of personal satire against some better and lesser known left wing figures (note Villette's characteristic posture) in a lively scene which recalls plates from the *Encyclopedie* illustrating workshop scenes.

121*

Untitled / *l'Ecclesiastique Réfractaire.*
Au milieu de l'Eclat le plus pur. Tu reste dans le Clair obscur.
Etching, hand coloured; Pl. 15, 1 x 22, 8;
Des. 14 x 18, 8;
Wtmk [letter T]
Unsigned, undated [1792]

This satirical portrait of a non juring priest still surrounded by the clouds of an obscurantist church has the incisiveness of line and the economy of design which are characteristic of large Italian caricatures, imitated by "élèves de Rome". The priest is silhouetted against the light by the effective use of black and brown on a white background. Yellow is used to contrast two symbolic representations, with the book (a missal?) providing the third point of an imaginary triangle, inside which the figure is inscribed. At his feet lie the signs of ecclesiastical authority. The triangle is often associated with other symbolic objects in Christian and masonic inscriptions. It may feature here as a symbol of the Supreme Being, but is more likely to be an allegory of Equality. Small compositions by Prud'hon, and an engraving by Savage dating from 1792 show characters in adoration in front of the radiating triangle of Equality. The cartoon may be primarily addressed to constitutional priests and designed to encourage them in their choice for the new democratic church. The satire is mild and there is some gentleness in the treatment of the profile.

122

Il ne nous reste que la fumée / le Depart de la Ste Famille
Etching, hand coloured; Pl. 17, 9 x 14, 3;
Des. 11, 9 x 16, 9;
Wtmk Pentacle (5, 6)
Unsigned, undated, [spring – early summer 1792]

The cartoon parodies one of the best-known genre-scenes of religious art, made familiar by many paintings and illustrated in cheaply produced prints decorating and sanctifying humble homes. In the iconographic tradition, *The Flight to Egypt* commonly shows the centre group (mother and child on a donkey) surrounded by attending angels with Joseph shown walking along the group. In a number of depictions Joseph carries a sack on his back or a sort of travel case in his hand, as do monk and bishop in this composition. The caption simply names the scene and underscores the satire: instead of saintly or holy figures it is the clergy which is shown leaving the land. The various types of clerics are identified by their vestments, dress, or habits, and further highlighted by denoting colours. In its general theme, the cartoon derides the emigration of the clergy, but the title points to a more specific message also conveyed in the picture by the group of small figures in red, unexpectedly added to the commonplace design: Three altar boys in red surplices swinging high their censers from which a cloud of incense smoke ('la fumée') rises. The clergy celebrate their own departure, as they have nothing left to celebrate, in a show of vanity - a point reiterated by the symbolic peacock (the fox and the goose symbolizing two other ascribed characteristics, guile and greed). To poke fun at the clergy's foible in particular their vanity is not new and hardly anti-clerical; even the mock-pageant is traditional. The iconographic theme is applied in an early cartoon (*Les Premiers Fuyards de la Révolution, 1789*) to the emigration of Artois, Poliguac and Condé. The use of the scene from the early life of the Lord to attack the clergy is closer to the bone. Moreover in giving mocking praise to their departure, the cartoon comes close to saying 'good riddance'.

Le Départ de la Ste Famille.

123

Untitled / GRAND COMBAT A MORT /
Caption in three columns:
1. Le Roi de Suede, 2. Le Roi de Prusse
retenant le Taureau avec des cordes. 3.
Le Roi de Boh}me attrapent à la volée la
Couronne de Marie-Antoinette que le
Taureau a fait sauter. 4. Le Comte
d Artois tuant le Taureau.
Aquatint and etching in grey; Pl. 18 x 14, 4;
Des. 16, 7 x 12, 1.
Wtmk : [Auvergne]
Unsigned [Michel Webert], undated
[June 1792; announced JCV 26.4.92]

The cartoon is designed to inspire compassion in a pro-royalist audience for
the personal plight of their queen, and
to elicit support for the Coalition by pre-
senting rulers and princes as personally
committed to protecting Marie Antoinette
and as moved by a spontaneous sense
of chivalry rather than by political mo-
tives. The plight of the queen is elo-
quently represented by the dramatic
image of a furious bull threatening a
helpless woman and by the menacing
high wall and turret of a fortress in the
right hand side background – strangely
similar to those of the *Temple*, where
the Royal family was later emprisoned.
Fidelity, allegiance and fearlessness are
strong aristocratic values which this cartoon seeks to stir in defense of royalty,
as the first anniversary of Varennes
approached. The central motif (bull-
fighting) would appeal to an aristocratic
audience who had become fond of
animal combats recently introduced by
Franconi amongst the acts of the fashionable circus established at Pantin, and
also to a wider public as the image
evokes traditional representations of the
martyrdom of Sainte Blandine.

124

Echantillon de l'Affaire de Mons / [on
two cols] DUO [left:] *le Soldat Patriote*
Jacobin AIR. *la Victoire / est a nous etc*
[right:] *le Soldat Patriote Feuillant* AIR
Qu'on se batte / qu'on se déchire / peu
m'importe
Key to character [left:] *1. Feuillant*
2. Houlan / [right:] *3. Talpache*
4. Jacobin.
Aquatint and dry point in black and
grey; Pl. 25 x 17, 4; Des. 22, 2 x 13, 6
Unsigned, undated [late May-early June
1792, stated as on sale in JCV 14.5.92]

On 29 April 1792, the French armies
who had moved into Belgium beat a re-
treat in front of the Austrian troops. The
cartoon is in the format of battle scenes
and shows an encounter between two
pairs of combatants in the foreground.
The title claims to 'give a taste' of what
took place at Mons when a French regiment retreated to the camp at Valenciennes, which had to be abandoned.
The dramatic gestures and postures are
characteristic of the genre and the military uniforms and weapons are accurately drawn (the *talpache* is a hungarian
light infantryman in the service of the
Emperor). The jacobin however stands
out in his civilian clothes and by his
posture of resistance (which is costing
him his arm). This apparently incongruous figure in battle and the symmetrical
composition of the two groups draws
attention to the political point of the
cartoon. It expresses the sense of shame
felt by many royalists at the humiliation
of the army on the frontiers, and point-
edly represents defeat as highlighting
the internal conflicts between the military and the ministry. In particular,
whilst the jacobins' minister of war
Dumouriez wished to pursue the offen-
sive, the pro-Feuillant generals meeting
at Valenciennes on 18 May refused to
do so and advised the King to sue for
peace.

1. le Roi de Suede.
2. le Roi de Prusse, retenant le Taureau avec des Cordes.

GRAND COMBAT A MORT.

5. la Reine de France renversée par le Taureau.

3. le Roi de Bohême attrapent a la volée la Couronne de marie Antoinette, que le Taureau a fait sauter.
4. le Comte d'Artois tuant le Taureau.

Echantillon de l'Affaire de Mons

le Soldat Patriote Jacobin
AIR.
la Victoire
est a nous. &c.
1. Feuillant 2. Houlan.

DUO

le Soldat Patriote Feuillant
AIR
Qu'on se batte
qu'on se déchire
peut m'importe
3. Valpache 4. Jacobin.

125

Untitled / Caption on two cols: [left] *J ai Ecarté les Coeurs; il a les piques, Et je suis Capot* [right] *Eh! bien! joues votre jeu.*
Aquatint and dry point in sepia; Pl. 28, 7 [cut]; Des. 20, 7 x 15, 1;
Wtmk [Auvergne] [17]78
Unsigned [Villeneuve?], undated [June-July 1792]

Bruel attributes this cartoon to Villeneuve, though it is not in his favoured black manner. The author is undoubtedly a skilled political cartoonist, aware of the appeal of familiar images for political propaganda. His plain speaking style is deliberately democratic in its appeal, though artistically cultured. The economy of lines achieves immediate comprehension; the visual register is simple, slightly jovial but without a hint of vulgarity. Connaisseurs would also have enjoyed the composition of genre scene (with a passing salute to Chardin) and the skillful execution in the manner of wash drawings. The game shown is piquet, and the subject matter selected lends itself admirably to the graphic expression of political comment. This 'King of games', a favoured one amongst the aristocracy, was essentially for two players. The stylishly discreet furniture alludes to the place of piquet as a society pastime for serious players (note nevertheless the subtle difference between the two chairs). Clothes and head-gear immediately identify the partners as King and sans-culotte, the two sides of the political powergame. The lack of any obtrusive detail or background focuses attention on the hands of cards held by the players. The King who has already discarded "hearts", is called upon to declare. Whoever has the longest suit will win. Louis now plays his *piques* ("spades") which the sans-culottes will take, thus completing all twelve tricks in spades and winning the game with a score of 40 (the King is *capot*). The caption helps the viewer to anticipate the end-game, and to savour

a political gamesmanship which foresees the victory of the sans-culottes over the King. The idea for this cartoon may come from a number of facetiae in the royalist newspaper Journal de la Cour et de la Ville and originally directed against d'Orléans. Having turned around the theme, the cartoonist puts it to the service of the sans-culotte cause.

126

PROPHETIE DES HONNETES GENS / LA CAUSE DES ROIS [under caption, key to cartoon] *La Victoire terassant les rebelles, 2 La Fay... 3 Rock...4. Luck... 5. La Paix ramenant l'abondance 6. Le Peuple*
Aquatint in grey dry point and etching; Pl. 28, 6 x 21, 2; Des. 24, 3 x 17, 3;
Wtmk Unsigned, undated, [Spring - early Summer 1792]

An eloquent piece of visual propaganda, in traditionalist style, in anticipation of royalist victory and in support of the Coalition. It addresses itself to 'honnêtes gens', i.e. well-born and well-bred people, at a time when French commanders on the verge of defeat privately advised Louis to seek peace, a move which angered the pro-war party in the Assembly and amongst ministers. The cartoon is in the manner of official commemorative prints, as sometimes commissioned by the Crown before the Revolution. It uses a circular composition along a garland of clouds, symbolically linking the cause of Kings to the welfare of subjects. The two allegorical groups also belong to the established pictorial imagery of Ancien régime propaganda: On the right, Triumph in the shape of a winged Victory sword in hand, crowning an obelisk with a crown of laurels (note the plaques bearing the names of the victorious princes and allies); on the left Peace reclining, her attributes those of Abundance (ears of corn, cornucopia) and Trade. Each group forms a coherent

vignette (à la Cochin fils); each makes its own political point. The people on the left are represented as subjects humbly and eagerly expecting a largesse from above. The French commanders crushed under the right hand side monument are designed for recognition (note their profiles, their sticks); the marching orders which they have dropped spell 'anarchie' and 'démocratie'. The unity of the representation is achieved by the semi circular framing which opens on to the illuminated scene in the background. The scene shown is that of an idealised sea-scape, of calm after the storm. The dioramic representation is further emphasized by a zodiac which shines like a rainbow over the scene and where crowned heads appear as in a shadow theatre — an added visual effect but also a prophetic sign heralding the victory of the cause.

J'ai Écarté Les Coeurs, | Eh! bien! joues votre jeu.
il a les piques,
Et Je Suis Capot.

PROPHETIE DES HONNETES GENS.

LA CAUSE DES ROIS.

1. La Victoire terrassant les rebelles, 2. la Foy... 3. Roch... 4. Luch... 5. la Paix ramenant l'Abondance 6. le Peuple.

la trinite Bourbonnaise / The caption is in the form of three songs, with words on 4 cols: [left] AIR: *Figaro Helas a quel triste sort / me reduit mon impuissance* [etc]. [middle] *Vive henri IV* [begins] *ministre: Inviolable Roi de France et d'Coblenz* [continues] *le Roi: oui ma pitance / est de plus d'un million;* [right] *Vive le Vin* [begins] *pour moi je suis de foi punique / je tiens le langage des Rois*
Aquatint, etching and dry point in black and grey; pl. 23, 9 x 21, 2;
Des. 22, 6 x 15, 6; Wtmk
Unsigned [Villeneuve]; undated [early June 1792]

The innovative design, the quality of execution and the use of black for background leave no doubt that the author of the cartoon is Villeneuve. It rivals in quality the best of right wing production, borrowing from it some of its satirical techniques, in particular in the combining of visual and verbal parody, but without the crammed allusiveness which often obfuscate the political point of right-wing satire. Villeneuve succeeds in producing a visually striking print, of rich ideological content. The real-size playing cards would immediately attract a large audience and draw them to tease out the political message hidden in the visual concatenation. The cartoon is intended to be deciphered both from left to right and up and down from card to medalion. Arranged in two horizontal bands, the images form two sequences of visual narrative, in parallel but contrasted themes and style, whose decoding is intended as a kind of political lesson, further illustrated in words in the caption. The playing cards are faithful reproductions of traditional court cards used at the time. The names Yvert and Delatre are those of well known contemporary *cartiers*. The medalions contain political vignettes illustrating aspects of Louis's recent career, treated in a satirical, allegorical and realistic vein. These different images are integrated into a single composition by the use of a black background. It creates a *trompe l'oeil* effect which makes the pictures stand out, as a tryptich displayed inside a darkened chamber. The arrangement ("le tableau") is intended to contrast traditional emblematic images of royalty, and views of the record of the monarchy before and during the Revolution. Villeneuve's aim is to debunk the sacredness of monarchy (The "Trinity") implicit in its traditional emblems and he does so by giving each of the traditional court card figures a visual counterpoint in the medalions. Political distancing is further strengthened by the effect of optical image created by the medalions, the true nature of the monarchy appearing so to speak under the magnifying glass of politics. The "Trinity" of court cards is thus compared with three historical incarnations of the King. The King of Clubs now stands for Louis the absolute monarch living off the land and his people ("trefle" means clubs, but also clover); the King of Spades ("piques" is also pikes) for the constitutional monarch installed by the nation, but rejecting his people (the cap and pike featured in the allegory): as the subcaption states, Louis could have ruled their hearts but through duplicity and gluttony, lost their respect (the third medalion shows him swearing with one hand, but drinking with the other, an image which anticipates the famous Tuileries scene of June 20th). The caption tells this tale in mock self apologetic verse: Louis still expects to be restored to his former power with the help of the 'Coblenz' princes, meanwhile he drinks away 'more than a million'. A small ironical inscription under the design, states that the "tableau" can be seen in the 'cabinet autrichien'). Caption and inscription give the immediate context which provided Villeneuve with his inspiration: On May 20th 1792 the King intervened in the affair of the *Comité autrichien*, a secret conspiracy alleged to be passing political and military information to the Coalition, and wrote to the Assembly on behalf of two of his ministers accused of involvement. Despite the suspicion in which he was held by many, the Assembly on June 1st granted him a substantial allocation on the Civil list. Villeneuve's cartoon, however, is not reactive or narrowly polemical, as many others. In his innovative design, which anticipates the political cartoon strip, he shows a flair for visual propaganda in the manner in which he 'turns around' popular iconography in order to demystify its latent ideology.

MARAT VAINQUEUR DE L'ARISTOCRATIE / DIOGENES *Couvert d'un bonnet rouge quitte son Tonneau pour donner la main a marat qui sort d'une Cave par le Soupirail* [below a dialogue:] *diogenes Camarade Sans-Culotte je t'ai cherché long-tems* MARAT *On persecutait la vérité je n'avais pas d'autre Asyle*
Aquatint, etching and dry point in black;
Pl. 19, 9 x 26,1; Des. 17, 4 x 20, 8
Signed "A Paris chez Villeneuve Graveur Rue Zacharie St Severin Maison du Passage No 72", undated [April-May 1793]

On 24 April 1793, Marat who had been indicted by the *Convention Nationale*, on a charge of undermining the authority of the Assembly, was acquitted by the Revolutionary Tribunal. As on such previous occasions, Marat was in hiding, printing his newspapers clandestinely in the basements of safe houses. On his acquittal he made a triumphant return to the Assembly. This print by Villeneuve celebrates his return and pays hommage to the Sans-culotte spirit. The design stages an encounter between Diogenes, the ancient philosopher and Marat, the "publiciste de la Republique française" (this is the new title given by Marat on March 1793, to his recent publication to avoid a banning order from the *Convention*). Across time, Diogenes, who according to Diogenes Laertius, went in search of a man, by the light of a lantern, lends a helping hand to Marat who comes out of his hiding place. The group fills almost the entire space. At each end of an oblique line, two familiar objects add to the sense of urban location and serve as metaphors for the ideals which the ancient philosopher and the modern publicist embody: The barrel recalls Diogenes's rebuff to Alexander the Great, the tethering stone, with broken chains refers to Marat's apology of freedom in his *Chains of slavery*, republished in 1792. The lantern, a symbol of enlightenment and revolution is at the centre of the image. Barrel, stone and lantern form the three points of a triangle which frames the symbolic gesture of the clasped hands, expressing comradeship. Movement is conveyed by the slight imbalance between the standing figure of Diogenes and the crouching posture of Marat, by an off centre perspective, and by the oblique line formed by the arms linking the two characters. The design integrates into an nocturnal street scene, neo classical, realistic and allegorical elements: note Marat's famous head gear, and the hydra of aristocracy held down by Diogenes whilst Marat crushes its heads. Visual unity is achieved by an atmospheric use of tone and by the strong architectural lines which frame the scene. All elements blend perfectly together to create a visual representation of the sans-culotte values (commitment to truth and comradeship), also voiced in the dialogue of the caption. Villeneuve's narrative allegory is a powerful testimony to the fusing of classical models and contemporary history which inspires the discourse of Revolutionaries.

Le Niveau National

Le Joli Moine
Profitant de l'occasion

Combat entre le Pere Duchêne et l'Abbé Caisse.
le Coup de Poing.

35*

l'Assembleé des Aristocrates, ou l'Harmonica des Aristocruches

Lancée et Vomissé S.te Pere tout ce que vous avés de plus noir dans l'esprit, invoquée les Demons pour qu'ils vous inspire tout ce qu'il y a de plus affreux, imité vos infame disciples qui se sont convert de tout les crimes les plus execrables et vous remplire par cela votre S.t Ministere, Mais la Nation Françoise craint peu vos foudres, et malgré toute votre malignité elle fera revivre, cherir et respecter cette S.te Religion que vos Satelites avoit avilie par la Cupidité et leurs infames debauche.

ah! Le Maudit animal il M'a tant Péné pour S'engraiser, il est Si gras,
qu'il en en est Ladre, je reviens du marché, je ne sais plus qu'en faire.

Retour de la Famille Royale, à Paris, le 25 Juin 1791.

Le chasseur pigmée de worms Envoié extraordinare
AM.ᵉ refugié à Mons.

Leçon donnée Par Ro........

C'est Semés des Perles devant les pourceaux

65*

84*   85*

TIENT VOILA MONSIEUR DEPIBALLE.

93*

Héritiers de la Constitution.

LES MALHEURS DE LA FRANCE, FURENT LEURS OUVRAGES.

La rage l'erreur et la cupidité enfantrent ces mons...s.

a. Chap..er biribi.
b. Targ..t.
c. Liecou..ux.
d. Cam..
e. Bar..ve.

f. Lam..th.
g. Guille..me.
h. Le Duc d'or...s.
i. La France.
k. Neker.

LE NOUVEAU CALVAIRE

TABLE DE
PROSCRIPTION
les trois Rohan
Condé Mirabeau
Bouille Lanberg
Broglie &c &c...

N.º 1. Louis seize mis en croix par les révoltés.

2. et 3. Monsieur et Mons.r Comte d'Artois freres du Roi liés par les Décrets des factieux [JJ] de ses motions régicides.

4. Robespierre a Cheval sur la constitution suivi de la gente Jacquine présente au bout d'une pique l'Eponge imbibée du fiel

5. la Reine accablée de douleur montre son epoux et ses frères et Sollicite une prompte Vangeance.

6. la Duchesse de Polignac au pied de la croix — M.gr le prince de Condé Indigné s'apprête a venger son Roi.

se vend a Paris chez, Webert Palais Royal galerie de bois N. 103.

119*

l'Ecclesiastique Refractaire.

Au milieu de l'Eclat le plus pur.
Tu reste dans le Clair obscur.

121*

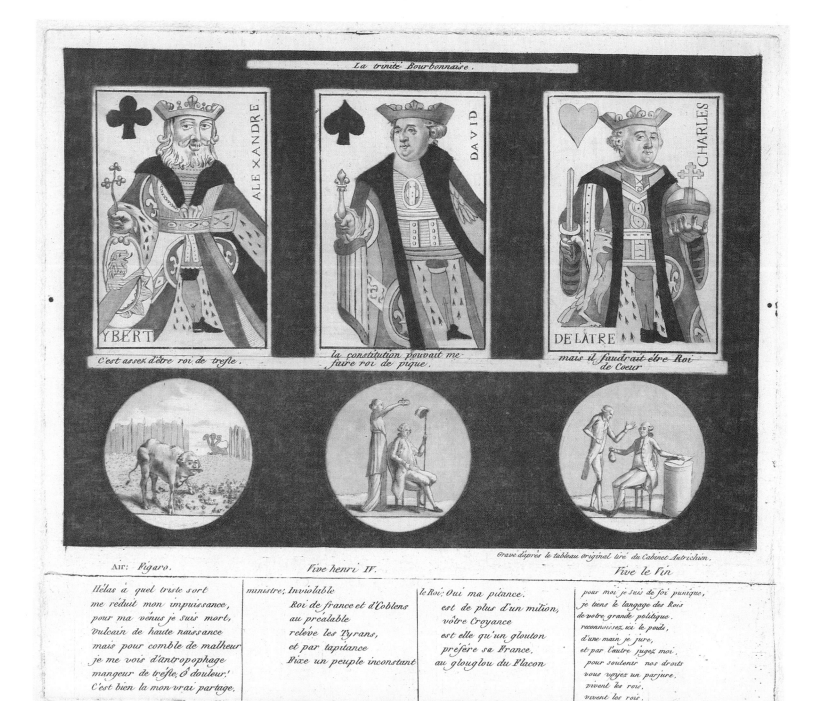

La trinité Bourbonnaise.

ALEXANDRE

DAVID

CHARLES

YBERT

DELATRE

C'est assez d'être roi de trefle.

la constitution pouvait me
faire roi de pique.

mais il faudrait être Roi
de Coeur

Gravé d'après le tableau original tiré du Cabinet Autrichien.

Air: Figaro.	Vive henri IV.		Vive le Vin
Hélas à quel triste sort me réduit mon impuissance, pour ma vénus je suis mort, Vulcain de haute naissance mais pour comble de malheur je me vois d'antropophage mangeur de trefle, Ô douleur! C'est bien la mon vrai partage.	ministre: Inviolable Roi de france et d'Coblens au prealable releve les Tyrans, et par tapitance Fixe un peuple inconstant	le Roi: Oui ma pitance. est de plus d'un million, vôtre Croyance est elle qu'un glouton préfère sa France. au glouglou du Flacon	pour moi je suis de soi punique, je tiens le langage des Rois de votre grande politique. reconnoissez ici le poids, d'une main je jure, et par l'autre jugez moi. pour soutenir nos droits vous voyez un parjure, vivent les rois, vivent les rois.

127*

MARAT VAINQUEUR DE L'ARISTOCRATIE.

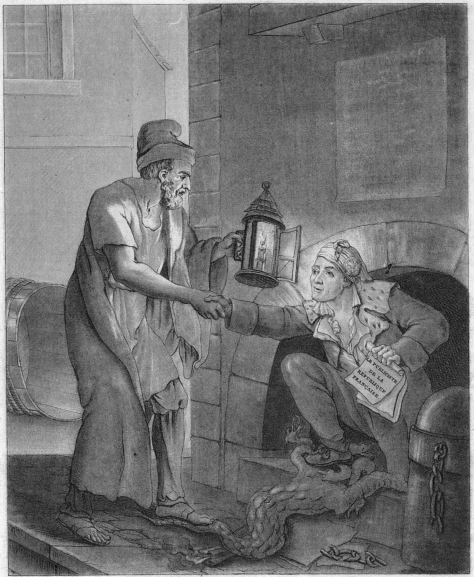

DIOGENES *Couvert d'un Bonnet rouge quitte son Tonneau pour donner la main à* MARAT *qui sort d'une Cave par le Soupirail.*

DIOGENES
Camarade Sans - Culotte je t'ai cherché long - tems

MARAT
On persécutoit la verité je n'avais pas d'autre Asyle.

A Paris chez Villeneuve Graveur Rue Zacharie S.t Severin Maison du Passage N.o 72.

NOTES